First Families Of McDonough & Henry County, GA Vol. II

Portions originally published under the title History of Henry County

Mrs. R.H. Hankinson 1921

First Families of McDonough & Henry County, GA

5th Printing – AUG 2014 1/0/5/0

Published by:
Eastern Digital Resources
31 Bramblewood Dr.
Cartersville, GA 30120
http://www.researchonline.net
EMAIL: Sales@Researchonline.net
Tel. (678) 739-9177

Contents

A Brief History of Henry County

The following record of Henry County's past was originally printed in 1921 as part of the celebration of the county's 100th birthday. With only a 100 year history, the author's perspective is itself near the origin of the county's birth. This perspective offers a unique look into the past.

Written by
Mrs. R.H. Hankinson

On May 15, 1921, Henry County will have reached its one-hundredth birthday. In celebration of this event, Henry County will be "At Home" to her children at McDonough on Saturday, May 14th. These children are many, for Henry County at one time embraced, in whole or in part, Spaulding, Dekalb, Fulton, Newton, Butts, Rockdale, Clayton, and Campbell Counties.

The land obtained from the Creek Indians by treaty on January 8th, was divided by an act of the legislature of May 15, 1821, into the counties of Henry, Houston, Monroe, Dooly, and Fayette. John Clark was the governor of Georgia. The county was named after Patrick Henry, of Revolutionary fame, thus spreading the mantle of distinction on it at its birth. This distinction was further contributed to, when on December 17, 1823, the county seat was incorporated and named in honor of the hero of the war so fresh in the minds and hearts of the people, Commodore McDonough, who on September 11, 1814, won such a brilliant victory over the British on Lake Champlain. Further distinction was given the county by naming the town of Hampton after the Hampton family, famous soldiers of South Carolina.

Traces of the Indian possession of the county are still found in the broken bits of pottery and arrow heads occasionally picked up, in such names as

Indian river, and Indian fisheries, and in a road known as the "Old McIntosh Trail" in Spaulding County, and which was the route followed by the Indians on their pilgrimages to and from the medicinal waters of Indian Springs.

Originally Henry County was about seventy miles square, and comprised eighteen land districts. It is now about twenty seven miles in length, and fifteen miles in width, and has one district left intact, the Seventh.

The earliest settlers came mainly from the counties of Morgan, Walton, Putman, and Jasper, and scattered over a broad area. The main point of entrance to the county was at the convergence of two Indian trails at a place on the Ocmulgee river, which was later given the name of Key's Ferry after one of the earliest settlers, a name which has since spread to a road through the county, and to a street through the county site. This road was part of the stage coach line between McDonough and Madison. The names of the earliest settlers included Glen, Strickland, Heflin, Woodward, Blissett, McClendon, Turner, Harper, Griffin, Grice, Green, Russell, Johnson, Brooks, Jackson, Malone, Weems, Armstrong, Beard, Patillo, McCally, Brown, Sims, Moseley, Abercrombie, Gay, Dearing, Callaway, Jenks. Eason, Kirk, Smith, Tuggle, Lovejoy, Key, Terrell, Shaw, Lasseter, Clayton,

Kimbrough, Pearson, Pate, Sellers, Wood, Barnes, Coldwell, McKnight, Patton, Steele, Stokes, Tye, Lemon, Speer, Price Nolan, Copeland, Carmichael, Berry, Ward, Stillwell, Markham, Cox, Wall, Crabbe, Clements, Brannan, Lowe, Campbell, Ray, Everett, Sloan, Stewtra, Peeples, Askew, Nolly, McDonald, Connell, Rodyhan, Terry, Setzer, Maxwell, Darbey, Hale, Goodwin, Pullin, Foster, Tidwell, Fargason, Varner, McDaniel, Bennett, Adams, Atkins, Tomlinson, Murray, Harris, Fears, Stockbridge, Sowell, Whittaker, Raven, and Crumbley.

Among the very first to come to the county were John Glen, Soloman Strickland and Wiley Heflin who settled on the Towaliga river. Aaron Woodward Elisha Blissit and Thomas McClendon came from Walton County about the same time, and settled on the Hampton road southwest of McDonough. Wade Turner and Roddy Harper went to the eastern part of the county and Mr. Hinton to Cotton Indian river. Mr. Frank Pearson, the progenitor of Mrs. Charles Bankston, of McDonough, settled east of McDonough, as did also William Wood. Thomas Russell came from South Carolina to McDonough. Jethro Barnes settled at Snapping Shoals, Jacob Hinton at Whitehouse, Parker Eason on the Towaliga river. John Dailey came from North Carolina to McDonough. Ezekiel Cloud came from Putnam in 1824. He was a distinguished Revolutionary soldier. Wade Turner came from Jasper

County. His brother Allen Turner was a Methodist preacher of prominence, who once came within one vote of being made a bishop. He was so fired with the zeal of his work that he would inquire about the spiritual welfare of everyone he met, and was frequently known to hold prayer services by the roadside with chance passers-by. The Clements family came from Virginia to McDonough. Benjamin and Barton Crabbe came from Wiles County. Samuel Weems settled near Bear creek. Elijah Foster, from whom Mrs. J. B. Dickson is a lineal descendent, came from Virginia and settled near Jonesboro. The Copelands came from South Carolina in 1826. John Stillwell came from Mecklenburg County, North Carolina. Dr. Tye accompanied him about 1830. William Berry came in 1836 and settled west of McDonough. John Crockett came in 1840. W. A. Stewart came from South Carolina with his parents in 1833, aged four years. Abel Lemon came from South Carolina to Georgia in 1813, and later entered Henry County. Alexander Price came from Virginia and settled near Flippen. His original home is still in possession of the family. John Cox came to McDonough in 1838, some years after his brother Oliver. John Ward came from Putnam in 1845 and settled at Lovejoy. Q. R. Nolan came in 1846, Miss Pamelia Campbell came in 1848 and settled in McDonough. J. M. Carmichael came in 1849, and settled west of McDonough. Thomas Speer came in 1852. Col. C. T. Zachary in 1854, A. R. Brown in 1873.

On December 24, 1821, an act was passed by the legislature which provided for the election of five justices of the inferior court who should define the militia districts of the county, provided for the election of the officers for the county site. William Harkins, David Castleberry, Cheedle Cochran, Soloman Strickland, William McKnight, Charles Gates, Sr., and Lee Jeffers were named as commissioners to hold the election for the justices. Henry was placed in the western circuit. The Flint Circuit had been created of the five new counties by the legislative act of December, 1824, to be effective after the next meeting of the legislature. To this circuit Dekalb, Bibb, Pike, Crawford, and Newton were attached later. This first session of the couth was held on June 10, 1822, at the home of William Ruff, Judge Augustus Clayton presiding. It was for Judge Clayton that Clayton County was later named, and McDonough still boasts lineal descendents of the illustrious old founder in the family of Mr. and Mrs. Jullian Weems. This session of court lasted one day. Another one-day session was held on December 9, 1822 – Henry County then belonged to the Flint Circuit. William Harden was clerk, and a Mr. Cook solicitor general pro tem. The first session of the inferior court was held in March, 1825, with William

Griffin, Garry Grice, Wade Turner, Joseph Green, and Thomas Russell presiding as justices, and Samuel Johnson serving as clerk. Cheedle Cochran was chairman of the first grand jury.

The first deed of record was drawn on March 7, 1822, between John and Mary Phillips, of Savannah and Thomas Elkins of land lot No. 71 in the Seventh district of Henry County. The first marriage was that of Bradford Hinton and Patience Lucre in November, 1822. Three marriages took place in the county during that year.

The first grist mill was erected by Jethro Barnes. Cattle raising was instituted in the county on a comparatively large scale for that day by Mr. Frank Pearson. A comparison of the taxes imposed on the citizens of Henry in that day with those of the present day reveals some interesting figures. Mr. Wade Turner paid taxes on two lots 202 1-2 acres each, four slaves and one poll, which amounted to the sum of $2.43. In 1837 the entire tax of the county $1,309.22, a sum less than some corporations and several individuals of the county now pay.

Agriculture was the leading pursuit of the early settlers, though corn and tobacco were raised more extensively than cotton because of the difficulty of separating the seed from the lint, and because it was not easy to secure gins. Game abounded throughout the county, and is remembered as being plentiful by even the oldest living citizens. A grog shop on the road near Locust Grove, called attention of passing planters, by a stuffed rattlesnake skin twined over the door, that thirst might be quenched within.

Religion came to Henry County with the first settlers. The first religious service was held at the home of Wade Turner. The first campground was laid off in the Rowan settlement. William Harden later donated the land for the Shingleroof campground to the Methodist Conference, and services are still held regularly at this place. It was in Henry County at a church in the Turner neighborhood that those differences, which had been existing for some time in men's minds first, were made public in 1825. These differences culminated in 1835 in Monroe County in a division, the branches of which were later as the Primitive and Missionary Baptist. In December, 1823, one acre was deeded to the Baptist, Methodist, and Presbyterian, each. The denominations carried the title of "Societies." The act that authorized the making of the deeds carried a provision that no cemetery should be laid off within three hundred yards of the Big Spring. This spring, located in McDonough, supplies water for the city of McDonough today. Mr. Gamble was the first Presbyterian, Mr. Cyrus White the first Baptist, and Mr. Bellah the first Methodist ministers of Henry County.

Four years later the town was incorporated. Tandy Key, Andrew Brown, William Clayton, James Kimbrough, and William Harden were named commissioners. McDonough was made from one half of lot No. 134, one half of lot No. 123, and one square lot of land, all in the Seventh district and purchased from Mr. Turner Evans. The site of the town was chosen with reference to the Big Spring. A courthouse was built of plank and cost $1,000.00. In 1824, there were five dry goods establishments in McDonough. They were owned by Clayton, Kimbrough, Shaw, Findley, and Hutcheson. There are seven such establishments now. The little daughter of Turner Evans was the first to die in the town, and was buried in the cemetery belonging to the old Presbyterian Church. A second cemetery was chosen on the old Methodist Church lot, but was moved to its present location to get it farther away from the Big Spring.

The first school was built of logs, and had a dirt floor. It stood on the hill above the Big Spring. The school was conducted by Mr. Fish. On December 12, 1853, a brick school house was built, and was called McDonough Collegiate Seminary. The trustees were Mr. Adam Sloan, Humphrey Tomlinson, Leonard Doyal, Thomas Speer, and Asa Brown. This building was destroyed by fire. The late Mrs. William Healey, of Atlanta, was one of the teachers in this building. She belonged to the Markham family. Mrs. Robert Lowery, of Atlanta is also a descendent of this family.

The county muster ground was near the present school house, and here the old Revolutionary soldiers met regularly to drill and reunion.

The first tavern was conducted by Tandy Key on the site occupied by McDonough Drug Company. It was a long house, built double. This was followed by Cox's tavern. Mrs. Enoch Callaway, of LaGrange, is a lineal descendent of the Cox family.

Among the early industries were a jug factory near Flippen, a brick plant near McDonough near the Tomlinson residence, an old tannery, opened by W. Tomlinson, and a silk factory, the last named being owned by John Dailey. Silk culture was not a success, and after a period of inoperation started as a cotton factory with one wing used for wool carding. The cotton was made into five pound hanks, and was sold to be knitted into clothing by hand. The factory later became a ginnery, and later a flower and corn mill. This building was washed away, but was rebuilt on the same site. This property is still in possession of the Dailey family. A nursery was also instituted by the Daileys and there are trees in the county now that were bought from this old nursery. Mr. Billy Beck introduced Bermuda grass into the county by way of the old Lemon estate. Mr. Minor started the first newspaper in 1828, the Jacksonian. It is claimed that is was the first newspaper in the United States to put the name of Andrew Jackson in nomination for the presidency. Here again Henry won historical distinction.

Even before Atlanta was built, McDonough was a town of considerable prominence. The development of the town was retarded because the old citizens and the town council objected to the entrance of the railroads, believing that they would bring with them objectionable features. Serving was actually done by the Central of Georgia Railroad, but because of the violent opposition, it was never built. Later on when railroads came to Griffin and Hampton, many people left McDonough and moved to these towns, tearing down their houses and hauling them with them.

Henry County lost land on all sides. On December 9, 1822, DeKalb County was made almost entirely from Henry. Fulton County was made from DeKalb in 1853. DeKalb also gave a portion of her land at an earlier date to Campbell County. In 1825 Butts County was created, and embraced a portion of Henry. In November, 1858 Clayton County was formed, and embraced a generous portion of Henry.

In 1870 Henry again made a contribution to Rockdale upon the creation of that county.

At the begging of the Civil War Henry was one of the leading counties in Georgia, and McDonough one of the leading towns in the middle part of the state. It lay in the region of greatest production, and consequently was of great importance to the Confederacy, a fact later attested to by its being included in Sherman's path of destruction on his way to the sea. The free population at this time was 9,759. The real estate was valued at $1,726,595.00 and the personal property at $2,869,342.00. The population now is $20,400, and the property valuation $7,372,599.00.

Many companies left Henry County during the Civil War. In all the county contributed about one thousand men to the cause. The first company organized, and the first to leave McDonough was under the command of Captain Flynt. The Lieutenants of the company were H. Stokes, J. R. Selfridge, and John R. Elliott. Captain Sloan led another company later. A part of the actual warfare was rought into the country towards the end of the conflict. After the battle of Atlanta, July 22, 1864, Kilpatrick's raiders made a visit to Henry under the direction of Sherman. Consternation seized the people. Men concealed themselves to prevent capture, and the women and children received the invaders and saw their cherished possessions thrown about in confusion, and their provisions destroyed at this time by the invaders. Many of the county records were also destroyed at this time by the invaders. Confederate forces under the command of General Ross and General Ferguson pursued these invaders, and overtook the last remnant of them to Cotton Indian river on Peachstone Shoals road. By leaving them no alternative, they forced them into the water where horses and wagons were lost and a number of soldiers were drowned.

Later Hood's Army with Wheeler's cavalry as advance guard, made a visit to Henry County and McDonough, and lighted the night with camp fires of twenty thousand soldiers. The battle of Jonesboro was fought next day, and the army moved on into Tennessee to threaten Sherman's line of supplies. On November 14, 1864, a wing of Sherman's army started to the sea by way of Jonesboro and McDonough. On the next day fighting took place between Jonesboro and Lovejoy. On November 16th, the enemy reached McDonough by way of Stockbridge, and left confusion and destruction in their wake. Here the army divided, a part leaving the county by the Macon road, and the other division leaving by the Key's Ferry road. A portion lost their way going down Peachstone Shoals road. Heavy rains came up, the river was flooded, and a number lost their lives in truing to cross. Names of prominence during this period were Sloan, Zachry, Ward, Hitch, Brown, Peeples, Elliot, and Farrar. After the surrender of Lee, General Stoneman entered the county with a body of soldiers in pursuit of President Davis.

During the period of Reconstruction, James Johnson was the provisional governor of Georgia. One of the features of this period most objectionable to the people of Henry County was the educational policy. The school system was directly under the control of the state. In 1872 the county system was again inaugurated, with Hon. Q. R. Nolan as first superintendent. In April, 1875, a resolution was passed by the grand jury that no more teachers should be elected from the colored schools of Atlanta because of objectionable teachings that had been traced to such teachers. A little later a gin and corn meal, the Baptist Church, and the McDonough Institute were burned. Out of such emergency the Ku Klux Klan was born. Its operations were confined principally to the eastern part of the county. Dave Fargason, a negro was killed. Those charged with the killing were arrested and imprisoned. The matter was adjusted by the Bureau Agent from Henry County, the appointment of Mr. George M. Nolan to the position, the turning over of the prisoners to the civil authorities of Henry County, and the promise of dissolution of the Ku Klux Klan in the county. The clan had existed from spring until fall of 1866.

Two chapters of the United daughters of the Confederacy have been organized in Henry County to preserve the history of this period and to do honor to the living, and keep bright the memory of the Heroes in Gray who have passed.

Since the war and the period of Reconstruction, Henry County has made steady progress. Henry is one of the most important agricultural counties of the state. The land is rich and productive, and is the farming is largely intelligent white farmers who live on the farms and look after their own work. Vegetables, fruits, grains, forage crops, and cotton are raised. The soil is particularly adaptive to the raising of cotton. A belt reaching from Stockbridge to the lower end of the county, and stretching entirely across, produces, according to local cotton men, a staple from an inch to an inch in quarter in length. McDonough cotton is known not only in domestic markets, but in foreign markets as well; and it demands a premium over other north Georgia cotton. The average yield for the county is between 25 to 30 thousand bales. The yield last year was about 28,000 bales. This fact establishes the productiveness of the county, for while other counties were cut short, Henry still produced a splendid yield.

The lack of manufacturing enterprises has been one of the serious handicaps to the county. However, advances have been made in this direction. The Hampton Cotton and Knitting Mill is a splendid enterprise, and particularly consumes all the cotton brought into the market. A guano factory has also been established at Hampton, which is meeting, if not shutting out, foreign competition.

A drainage project near Stockbridge is increasing the cultivatable area by hundreds of acres, and adding materially to the wealth of the county. A main canal sixteen miles in length, beginning at a width of 25 feet, and increasing to 42 feet, and eight feet deep, is being dug at a cost of $100,000.00. The Morris Construction Co., of Marietta, is in charge, and are using two dredges in the construction of the ditch. Pates creek, Rum creek, and Big Indian creek are in the line of activity.

One of the recently acquired industries is the Grist Mill and Ice Factory of McDonough, managed by Mr. Fred Varner, and known as the Henry County Milling and Ice Company.

There is considerable water power in the county, most of which up to date has remained undeveloped. Dr. J. G. Smith has built a dam on Cotton Indian river completed about a year ago, which supplies power for lights and other purposes for McDonough and vicinity.

Henry County has had local tax for a number of years, and its rural schools are in good condition. Recently $1,500.00 state aid has been secured for a county high school for next year, adding to the importance and the efficiency of the McDonough school. Locust Grove Institute is one of the most important secondary schools of the state. Prof. Claude Gary has patronage from all sections of the state. Locust Grove Institute is regarded not only as a fine institution, but as a school of splendid ideals.

Henry County does not lie in a mineral belt, however, mica has been found, and development has been begun on a farm by Mr. Fillmore Bowden. A rock quarry near Stockbridge produces an excellent quality of gray granite.

Henry County has eight banks with resources amounting to one and three-quarter million dollars.

Henry County played her part in the World War by sending volunteers and filling her quota in the draft. A number of her sons rose to positions of rank, and seven made the supreme sacrifice. They were Sergeant Troy Barret, Claude Babb, Corp. James A.

Davis, Corp. Tom F. Gardner, William Mayo, B. F. Moseley, E. N. Williams.

The Red Cross was particularly active, and the spirit of patriotism was maintained by the subscriptions to the Liberty loans.

There are in Henry County five branches of the Georgia Federation of Women's Clubs and four men's organizations – Masons, Oddfellows, Woodmen, and Knights of Pythias.

The Southern Railroad, which came in 1882, passes through the entire length of the county, and offers splendid schedules between Macon and Atlanta. This road was formerly called the East Tennessee, Virginia and Georgia railroad. This road had been surveyed through Jasper County. Mr. W. F. Smith, of Flovilla, in order to have the road pass through his town, with the assistance of Mr. Nolan, of McDonough, brought such pressure to bear on the officials of the road, that its course was diverted from the route originally proposed, to the present one, which passes through Henry County. Later another road was built connecting Columbus and McDonough. This road is now a part of the Southern system.

The roads of Henry County have gradually been improved until they are now in fairly good condition. Under the present arrangement of co-operation between state and national governments, the Dixie Highway, which passes through the county, has been put into excellent shape.

With lands that are fertile and productive, with an intelligent and industrious citizenship, the county's growth and prosperity are assured.

By Mrs. R. H. Hankinson

The Historical Pageant

On Saturday, May 14, 1921 at 9: AM, on the "Assembly Ground" at Keys' Ferry Road, the celebration began to mark Henry County's 100th Birthday. It was a grand occasion requiring much preparation and receiving the attention and support of the community. The schedule of activities that follows, is a duplicate of the first two pages of the booklet entitled, History of Henry County; published as a guide for the events of the day and as a documentation of Henry County's 100 year history. Wiley A. Clements, the booklets publisher, recognized Miss Emily Griffin and Mrs. R. H. Hankinson, for their contribution. The Pageant event schedule is duplicated below.

By

Annie Nolan

Chairman of the Pageant

History Of Henry County
Historical Pageant

Saturday, May 14, 1921, 9 A. M.

Assembly Ground, Keys' Ferry Road

1. Hearalds with Silver Horns.

2. Locust Grove Institute Band.

3. Colors with Military Escort.*

4. Locust Grove Institute Battalion.

5. Goddess of Henry.

6. Signing of the Treaty, General McIntosh and Creek Indians.

7. Patrick Henry, for whom the County Was Named.

8. Commodore McDonough, for whom the County Seat Was Named.

9. Wade Hampton, for whom Hampton Was Named.

10. First Mode of Travel – Ox Cart.

11. Second Mode of Travel – Pillion.

12. Descendents of All Families, 1821 to 1850. A number of Cars.

13. First Session of Superior Court, June 10, 1822.

Augustus Clayton, Judge; William Harden, Clerk; William Cash, Solicitor-General Pro Tem. 14. Second Session of Superior Court, December 1822.

Eli S. Shorter, Judge; Major Chettle Cochran, Foreman. 15. First Session of Inferior Court March, 1825. William Griffin, Gary Grice, Wade H Turner, Joseph P. Green and Thomas C. Russell acting as Justices and Samuel Johnson acting as Clerk.

16. Replica of the House in Which the First Religious Service Was Held. Log Cabin near Turner Church, built by Wade H. Turner, January 15, 1882.

17. First Methodist Circuit Rider, Mr. Bellah.

18. First Baptist Preacher, Mr. Cyrus White.

19. First Presbyterian Preacher, Mr. Gable, 1826.

20. First School Teacher, Mr. Fish, 1823.

21. First Factory, Dailey's, 1824.

22. First GristMill, Dailey's 1884.

23. Early Settlers.

24. Old Fashion Costumes, Belles of Other Days.

25. Plantation Float, Black Mammy and Banjo Days.

26. Veterans of the Sixties.

27. Ku Klux Klan – Reconstruction Days.

28. U. D. C. Floats, 1905, Children of The Confederacy Float.

29. Central of Georgia Railroad, First Railroad in Georgia. First Railroad in Henry County.

30. Southern Railroad, June 3, 1882.

31. King Cotton Float.

32. Corn Float.

33. Bank of Henry County, First Bank, June 23, 1896.

34. First Telephone, About 1897.

35. Southern Bell Telephone and Telegraph Co., 1900.

36. Electric Light Float, August, 1912.

37. World War Float, Army and Navy With Liberty Escort of ex-Service Men of Henry County – 1914 to 1918.

38. Red Cross Float, 1914.

39. Hampton, Red Cross Ambulance With Wounded Soldier.

40. Locust Grove Red Cross – "The Greatest Mother in the World".

41. McDonough Red Cross – Red Cross Army Supplies With Red Cross Nurses – 1914.

42. Womens Club, 1916 – The Federation of Clubs Will Be Represented by several cars.

43. Bells of 1921 – Floats.

44. Floats of Manufacturing Companies and Other Industries – A Number of Cars.

45. Masons of the County.

46. Woodmen of the World.

47. Knights of the Pythias.

48. Red Men.

49. Town Councils.

50. Schools of the County.

Annie Nolan,

Chairman of the Pageant

Hampton and Her History

The following record of *Hampton and Her History* was printed in 1921. Taking her part in the celebration of Henry County's 100th birthday, the author gives special attention to the details of Hampton's origin and developmental accomplishments. This detail offers a unique look into *Hampton and Her History.*

Written by Miss. Emily Griffin

Hampton and Her History

By Miss Emily Griffin
1921

Two surveyors once lay down to rest from the heat of the noonday's summer sun near a cool spring beneath the shade of two magnificent poplars. Shading his face from the glare of the sun's rays, one of the men raised his eyes to the branches of the larger tree and, with a smothered exclamation, he jumped to his feet and grabbed his gun; for, sitting calmly upon a limb and each in the act of "surveying" the surveyors, sat two great, black bears!

The village, which was being laid off, had up to this time, received no name, but in the future, because of the bears which inhabited the banks of the creek, it was to become known as Bear Creek, Ga.

The first building erected was in the year, 1848. "Lowery's Store" and the Postoffice were in this same building and was for two years the gathering place for the male inhabitants of the village.

For the next three years the village of Bear Greek continued to grow and prosper and it was decided to move it to a more convenient spot where the best interests might have the greatest advantages. So in

1851 Bear Creek moved half a mile in a southeasterly direction.

Among the first settlers in Bear Creek were: Messrs. Tom Barnett, who succeeded Lowery as postmaster and who was also a merchant; Jim Hightower and Pete Knight, Lem and Ben Roan, Cas Black, another merchant, and Gray Hughes, the shoemaker. These settlers' homes were in the village and they are the pioneers who first promoted the civic improvement of Bear Creek.

The men whose plantations formed the circle that skirted the village of Bear Creek were: T. J., J. L,, and Jim Edwards, Jim Cleveland, Buck Fears, Wade Westmoreland, Smith II. Griffin, George Barnett, R. A. Henderson, R. A. Moore, R. W. Turnipseed, and John H. Smith. The descendants of nine of these old families are living on the original sites of these old homesteads today.

As time passed on and the village became known over the state, Bear Creek, after the perversity of her sex, decided to change her name. It was fitting that a name more in keeping with the new spirit of thrift and advancement should be accredited the little village which had now reached the size of a small town. So a meeting was held and at the suggestion of one of the residents. Rev. Smith H. Griffin, it decided to re-name Bear Creek and call it Hampton, after Gen. Wade Hampton.

Bear Creek had been incorporated in 1872, so by an amendment of the charter, which was in the year, 1873, she became known as Hampton, and Mr. Thomas Barnett, the justice of the peace, was elected mayor, and Hampton proper started on a career that she can be justly proud of.

As "a chain is no stronger than its weakest link", so is a town or community no stronger that its schools. Realizing this fact, Hampton was maintaining a school whose boys and girls were being taught by Judge Mitcham, father of Mr. A. B. Mitcham. Judge Mitcham can be reckoned as an empire builder whose work was of lasting benefit. "The Pine Grove Masonic Lodge Building" was used for the school house and was situated beneath the giant oak on the lawn of Mrs. Irene Henderson.

In 1851 the Central of Georgia had built her road that came through Hampton. This, of course, had been the greatest thing done for the business interests of the town. Since it was the only railroad in the section, until the Southern railroad was built in a neighboring town, Hampton was the center of every business activity within a radius of forty miles. All the cotton in surrounding counties was shipped from Hampton over the Central to its destination.

The depot at Hampton was then in the center of the town and opposite the building now occupied by The First National Bank. The first agent was Mr. Bill Adair.

Hotels sprang up after the building of the railroad and the first one was owned by John Turnipseed and Ben Thompson, and was under the management of Ben Thompson. Another hotel of that time was the McIntosh Hotel.

The houses of worship, in order of their establishment, were: First—the Primitive Baptist, the Protestant Methodist, the Christian Church, and the Baptist Church. These churches are all represented today in the town, except that the Methodist Episcopal has taken the place of the Protestant Methodist. The Christian Church is a monument to the memory of "Uncle Buck Fears," who built it and who was its pastor for years. Besides these Hampton has four negro churches.

In 1875 occurred the greatest financial boom that Hampton has known. This was the year that George Schaeffer, sent down by Atlanta cotton buyers, was stationed at Hampton; and it was no uncommon sight to see hundreds of wagons of cotton standing in the road along the railroad waiting to be disposed of and then sent down the road for other interests.

Situated in the midst of the richest cotton section it was but natural that manufacturing industries should spring up, and on May 17, 1900, the Hampton Cotton Mills were incorporated. Mr. A. J. Henderson, a wide-awake and energetic citizen started the company that grew and prospered and which at his death, three years ago, was one of the most solid business institutions of its kind in the state. The original capital $50,000.00 and the following directors were elected: President, A. J. Henderson; Vice President, W. P. Wilson; Secretary and Treasurer, W. M. Harris; R. J. Arnold, H. G. Fields, J. L. Moore, and R. F. Smith.

Other original stockholders were P. W. Pullin, J. T. Lewis, and Mrs. Thomas McMahon. In 1904 the capital stock was increased to $100,000.00 and in 1908 was again increased to $150,000.00. In 1917 A. J. Henderson resigned and W. M. Harris was elected president and R. M. Harris, secretary and treasurer. In 1919 its capital stock was increased to $300,000.00 and the plant of Henderson Manufacturing Company was bought. In January, 1920, R. 0. Arnold was elected a director with office of secretary and treasurer and R. M. Harris elected superintendent and general manager. In July, 1920. W. M. Harris resigned as president and R. 0. Arnold was elected president. The present officers and directors are, R. O. Arnold, President; W. P. Wilson, Vice President; R. M. Halo-is, Superintendent and General Manager; W. M. Harris, Chairman Board of Directors; J. L. Moore, H. O. Fields, J. M. Tarpley, and C. V. Williams.

The Hampton Cotton Mills has 1,400 spindles and 41 knitting machines, and 25 sewing machines. They manufacture soft and hard yarns and ladies' underwear. Also operate an ice plant with a capacity of five tons daily. The mills consume about seven or eight thousand bales of cotton annually and employ about two hundred and fifty people.

Besides the mills, Hampton has other industries that are growing. One is a Foundry, which is "owned and operated by Messrs. Arthur and Jim Henderson, both sons of the late A. J. Henderson. The Hampton Milling Company makes both plain and self-rising flour and also has a bleachery for patent flour. In this same plant is a corn mill which is run by electricity.

The Planters Warehouse and Gin Company also ran a grist mill. The Fertilizer Plant, or the Porter Fertilizer Works have a capacity of fifteen thousand tons per year.

The light and water system of Hampton is of the very best. The two deep wells furnish the water supply of Hampton; and it is given up by insurance companies that Hampton has the best water and fire equipment of any town.

The two banks are. The Bank of Hampton and The First National Bank.

The Bank of Hampton was organized and opened for business October 1, 1902, with a paid in capital of $25,000.00. The following were the incorporators: A. J. Henderson, Dr. R. J. Arnold, W. P. Wilson, Smith H. Griffin, W. M. Harris, J. C. Tarpley, W. D. Henderson, J. L. Moore, and I. D. Crawford. The first officers of the bank were, W. P. Wilson, President; Smith H. Griffin, Vice President; J. O. Norris, Cashier. Since the organization, the bank has paid out in cash dividends to the stockholders $57,000.00. The book value of the stock is at the present more than $300.00 per share.

There are few banks in Georgia that have done better than The Bank of Hampton. In fact, it is considered by leading bankers, business men, and state officials as one of the best all-round banks in the State of Georgia. It has always been the policy of the bank to be conservative, yet liberal in its dealings so long as consistent with sound banking. There is no bank that appreciates its good customers more than The Bank of Hampton.

The following are the present officers and directors of the bank: W. P. Wilson, President; David J. Arnold, Vice President; J. O. Rutherford, Cashier; Miss A. L. Rutherford, Assistant Cashier. Directors: W. P. Wilson, David J. Arnold, J. M. Tarpley, J. O. Rutherford, H. G. Fields, H. T. Moore, and J. L. Moore.

The First National Bank of whom W. M. Harris-is President opened for business on November 14, 1911, with a paid in capital of $30,000.00; surplus $3,000.00. The first officers were: President. W. M. Harris; Vice President, A. M. Henderson and E. R. Harris, Cashier. The directors were: W. M. Harris, A, M. Henderson, E. R. Harris, R. E. Henderson, R. M. Harris, W. W. Carmichael, and T. G. Barfield. The present capital is $50,000.00; surplus and undivided profits $40,000.00. As stated W. M. Harris is the President, T. G. Barfield. the Vice President, and E. R. Harris, Cashier. Directors of this bank are: W. M. Harris, R. E. Henderson, R. M. Harris, H. M. Lovern, T. E. Lindler, R. O. Tarpley, and John B. Weldon.

One of the best schools for any town of its size in the state, is the Hampton Public School. Mrs. Lucy P. Richard, who was for ten years connected with the

Georgia Military College, has proven an able and efficient principal for the past three years, and through her suggestion and the efforts of the town at large, it is hoped that September will find the High School enlarged by an additional class. Fostered by the Woman's Club the campus has been beautified and playground equipment procured and the building and grounds are a source of pride to every resident of the town.

Although not every farmer in Hampton is a merchant, yet most every merchant is a farmer. The oldest merchant - though not the oldest man-in Hampton, is J. C. Tarpley. Next in service as a merchant is Hamp Moore. These two have been in business on Main Street in the town for over twenty-five years.

Two of the most modern drug stores in the county are: Cain's Pharmacy and The Service Drug Store.

One of the most up-to-date stores in Hampton is that of H. T. Moore & Company, which is owned and operated by H. T. Moore and "The Moore Boys," Messrs. Arnold, Frank, and Norman Moore. This business house occupies two street fronts and is equipped with style and furnishings with a view to both beauty and service.

Among the other merchants of Hampton are: H. M. Lovern, D. G. Hawkins, W. A. North, The Crescent Mercantile Company owned by Messrs. Moore and Peeples, The Hampton Hardware and Furniture Company owned by L. J. and E. C. Copeland, Henry Hand, and J. L. Turnipseed. The latter is the son of John W. Turnipseed, a pioneer of Hampton.

Some of the prettiest homes in Henry County are those in and around Hampton. Among these may be mentioned the homes of J. L. Moore, A. B. Mitcham, W. M. Harris, Roy Harris, Will Art Wilson, Mrs. Irene Henderson, W. P. Wilson, Henry Moore, Will Edwards, Rome Moore, Robert Peeples, and Jim Minter. Two old homesteads are: The Edward's home, which is west of Hampton and the property of Lemmie Edwards; and "Oaklea," the home of Charles H. Griffin and which was built by his father, Smith H. Griffin. "Oaklea" is east of Hampton on the "Middle McDonough road," and was the scene of many a runaway marriage during the lifetime of Rev. S. H. Griffin.

Hampton District is possessed of unlimited, undeveloped water power. It all has lain in reserve except that which the Georgia Railway and Power Company get from the Towaliga River that heads two miles of Hampton. As yet we only dream of the possibilities contained in the streams that flow between the emerald banks.

It has been said that "History is a drama enacted upon the theater of time," and indeed it is. From the first characters, from the first mayor who presided in the early, days of Bear Creek up to now when our mayor, Mr. J. L. Pritchett, and his efficient Council play their parts in the story of our town, our history has been an unbroken, uninterrupted story with characters and acts befitting the drama which is constantly becoming bigger, better and quicker of action. It is the hope of every Hamptonian, that as the years glide by they, too, may leave works that will make the history of the next hundred years as full of benefit and promise as did the faithful ones whose work they now carry on.

By Miss Emily Griffin
1921

History of Locust Grove

By Miss. Emily Griffin

From the best available information it appears that Locust Grove derived its name from a beautiful grove of flowering locust trees around the home of William Carroll, which later became the old home place of Rev. R. F. Smith. It was in Carroll's store that the first postoffice at Locust Grove was kept.

About 1846 Carroll sold out to William Kimbell. Kimbell kept the postoffice in his home, which -was also operated as a tavern and a place for the accommodation of mule and hog drovers who were numerous in those days. In 1864 Kimbell moved to Louisiana, selling to George P. Combs, Sr., who, with Alexander Cleveland, operated the first blacksmith shop in the place.

About 1847 Math Tidwell built what is known as the Hamp Dickens home. One room of his dwelling was used as a store. About 1852 he sold to Harrison Speer, who built rather a large house which was used as store, postoffice, and shoe shop.

Prior to this time Mount Gilead was a prosperous Methodist Church located on the site of the present campus of Locust Grove Institute, but which has now gone down. Speer being a devout Methodist gave a site for a new church on the lot where is now the home of Tom Barnett. He, Dick Stillwell, and Charles Barker erected a building and re-organized the church. In 1907 the church was moved to its present location and a handsome concrete building was erected:

In 1869 Harrison Speer sold out to H. B. Dickson, who kept a store in his residence the old Tidwell home. He was the first to operate a public gin in the town, which was an old-fashioned horse-power affair. The first steam gin was operated by Bill Colvin and R. F. Smith in 1874.

The Indian Creek Baptist Church was founded in 1826. It was then located about two and one-half miles south of Locust Grove on the A. W. Walker place. In 1862 during the pastorate of J. G. Kimbell, it was moved to the present site of the Locust Grove Baptist Church. The present church house was erected in 1916-17. From the devotion of the cause of education of one of its pastors. Rev. B. J. W. Graham, and the money and sacrifice of its members came the Locust Grove Institute, which has meant so much to the community and which has blessed the lives of more than 3,000 boys and girls all over the South.

The first school was taught in 1850 by James Crowley in old Mount Gilead Church, which stood just west of the present site of the boys' dormitory. He was followed for several terms by Robert Sandifer. In 1858, on the home place of Arch Brown, just east of the present town, there was erected a pretentious building for those times which went by the name of Locust Grove Academy, and which, for several years, enjoyed considerable local fame as an educational institution. In 1866 the Locust Grove members of the Ringgold Masonic Lodge, of Spalding County, were granted a dispensation to form a new lodge. This new lodge room was built above the old academy.

A few years later a small one-room house was built on the spot where the present cottage now stands and school was held in this for several years. After the coming of the Southern Railroad the Masons moved the old academy and lodge building and added it to this one-room building. In a very few years it became necessary to add another and larger room to the front of this lodge and school room. In 1894 the first building of Locust Grove Institute was erected on an adjacent lot just north of the cemetery and the old school building was used as a dormitory for boys. It is interesting to note that the educational interest of Locust Grove through all the years has centered in and revolved around the very spot now occupied by Locust 'Grove Institute.

Just east of the present town site in 1870, Arch Brown ran a store, a blacksmith shop a wood shop, and a shoe shop.

With the coming of the railroad J. B. Dickson built the first store on what is now Main Street. The first cotton warehouse was built by George Schaeffer in 1882 on the spot now occupied by the Planters' Warehouse. In 1883 Arch Brown built a concrete store house on the main street with a blacksmith shop on the rear of the lot. He also put an up-to-date public gin, using a new 10-horse power steam engine. The store has been twice burned but the walls are still standing and the place is occupied by the Leslie-George Pharmacy. A year or two later, 1885, Arch Brown moved his dwelling house from its old site, about a half mile east of town, living in it during the process of moving. The old house is still standing. It has been remodeled and is now the handsome home of Dr. E. G. Colvin.

The first brick store was built by A. H. Price and is now occupied by Hubbard & Pitts. The first bank, the bank of Locust Grove, was organized in 1902 by F. S. Etheridge, of Jackson and Atlanta. The original building burned, but was immediately rebuilt on the same spot.

In 1889 S. B. Kimbell, with local capital, organized and erected the Farmers' Cotton Oil Company, which later was sold to the Southern Cotton Oil Company. The buildings are still standing and are operated by the Henry County Gin Co.

The later developments in the life of Locust Grove are so modern that no record now is needed.

History of the Locust Grove Institute

by Miss. Emily Griffin

Locust Grove Institute was founded in 1894 by the Flint River Baptist Association through the special efforts of Rev. B. J. W. Graham. The original trustees were T. R. Mills, G. W. Garner, G. W. Good, A. W. Walker, T. W. O'Kelley, I. G. Walker, J. H. Mitchell, E. Culpepper, F. S. Etheridge, R. F. Smith, D. W. Scott, W. T. Kimsey, J. R. Williams, J. W. Beck, and A. G. Combs. There are now eleven Baptist associations affiliated with the Flint River Association in sponsoring the educational work at Locust Grove. These associations are the Atlanta, Western, Columbus, Central, Kimball, Stone Mountain, South River, Centennial, Pine Mountain, Fairburn, and Morgan County Associations.

With Prof. Y. E. Bargeron as principal and Miss Hester Mae Walker as assistant the first session opened with 13 pupils on November 1, 1894, in a brick store room of Rev. R. F. Smith. During the three years of able management of Professor Bargeron the attendance increased to 156. For the first three years the equipment consisted of a large wooden main building and a 30x50ft old school room with no partitions and in which the president and the boys had their beds side by side in one end and in the other end did their cooking. Less than $5.00 per month covered the cost of board at that time.

Upon the resignation of Professor Bargeron in 1897, Prof. Claude Gray was elected president and has continued to the present time.

From a two-acre lot, a wooden main building and an old school room as dormitory, the equipment has increased until now the campus contains 47 acres of land upon which are four cottages, two large brick dormitories, and a handsome brick administration building with total valuation of more than $125,000.00. The teaching force has grown from two members to a splendid faculty of eighteen. The following departments of instruction are represented: Literary, Music, Expression, Commercial, Domestic Science, Art, Bible, Military, and Athletics.

The patronage has increased from 13 on the opening day to 289 last year, of which 243 were boarders. Georgia furnishes a majority of its students, but 15 states and 4 foreign countries have been represented in its student body. On its rolls have been 727 from Henry County. The names of more than 3,000 pupils are on its records. Among these have been 133 ministerial students; 273 teachers, and 662 who have been prepared for and have entered the colleges of this and other states. Nearly 200 pupils have been converted and have joined the church during their school days here.

Locust Grove Institute was among the first of the Georgia preparatory schools to be placed on the accredited list of the Association of Schools and Colleges of the Southern States. Pupils who graduate here have for many years been accepted without examination by the leading colleges of America. For nearly fifteen years pupils have been successfully prepared for the Sophomore Class at college.

In 1914 a splendid recognition was given Locust Grove Institute by the Commission of International Conciliation. Seven co-educational preparatory schools were selected to represent the leading denominations of America. Locust Institute was chosen to represent the Baptist schools of this class.

In 1918 38 per cent of the students who entered the Georgia colleges from the high schools of Georgia failed on one or more courses. Out of thirty pupils who entered the Georgia colleges from Locust Grove Institute in 1917 and 1918 there was only one who made a failure.

An extensive program of enlargement has begun which contemplates an expenditure of more than two hundred thousand dollars in buildings and equipment and. one hundred thousand dollars in endowment. This program of enlargement was begun last fall by the erection of a new dormitory for boys at a cost of $25,000.00. A new athletic field is now under construction and will be ready for the fall term opening. Architect drawings have already been accepted for a handsome building to be erected by the Alumni. This building will provide a large auditorium, society halls, library, and studios for music, expression and art, and quarters for the domestic science department. Other buildings will be added as needed.

The Baptists of Georgia propose to make Locust Grove Institute the best equipped preparatory school in all the South.

Written by Miss. Emily Griffin
in 1921

Hampton and Her History

By Miss Emily Griffin
1921

Two surveyors once lay down to rest from the heat of the noonday's summer sun near a cool spring beneath the shade of two magnificent poplars. Shading his face from the glare of the sun's rays, one of the men raised his eyes to the branches of the larger tree and, with a smothered exclamation, he jumped to his feet and grabbed his gun; for, sitting calmly upon a limb and each in the act of "surveying" the surveyors, sat two great, black bears!

The village, which was being laid off, had up to this time, received no name, but in the future, because of the bears which inhabited the banks of the creek, it was to become known as Bear Creek, Ga.

The first building erected was in the year, 1848. "Lowery's Store" and the Postoffice were in this same building and was for two years the gathering place for the male inhabitants of the village.

For the next three years the village of Bear Greek continued to grow and prosper and it was decided to move it to a more convenient spot where the best interests might have the greatest advantages. So in

1851 Bear Creek moved half a mile in a southeasterly direction.

Among the first settlers in Bear Creek were: Messrs. Tom Barnett, who succeeded Lowery as postmaster and who was also a merchant; Jim Hightower and Pete Knight, Lem and Ben Roan, Cas Black, another merchant, and Gray Hughes, the shoemaker. These settlers' homes were in the village and they are the pioneers who first promoted the civic improvement of Bear Creek.

The men whose plantations formed the circle that skirted the village of Bear Creek were: T. J., J. L,, and Jim Edwards, Jim Cleveland, Buck Fears, Wade Westmoreland, Smith II. Griffin, George Barnett, R. A. Henderson, R. A. Moore, R. W. Turnipseed, and John H. Smith. The descendants of nine of these old families are living on the original sites of these old homesteads today.

As time passed on and the village became known over the state, Bear Creek, after the perversity of her sex, decided to change her name. It was fitting that a name more in keeping with the new spirit of thrift and advancement should be accredited the little village which had now reached the size of a small town. So a meeting was held and at the suggestion of one of the residents. Rev. Smith H. Griffin, it decided to re-name Bear Creek and call it Hampton, after Gen. Wade Hampton.

Bear Creek had been incorporated in 1872, so by an amendment of the charter, which was in the year, 1873, she became known as Hampton, and Mr. Thomas Barnett, the justice of the peace, was elected mayor, and Hampton proper started on a career that she can be justly proud of.

As "a chain is no stronger than its weakest link", so is a town or community no stronger that its schools. Realizing this fact, Hampton was maintaining a school whose boys and girls were being taught by Judge Mitcham, father of Mr. A. B. Mitcham. Judge Mitcham can be reckoned as an empire builder whose work was of lasting benefit. "The Pine Grove Masonic Lodge Building" was used for the school house and was situated beneath the giant oak on the lawn of Mrs. Irene Henderson.

In 1851 the Central of Georgia had built her road that came through Hampton. This, of course, had been the greatest thing done for the business interests of the town. Since it was the only railroad in the section, until the Southern railroad was built in a neighboring town, Hampton was the center of every business activity within a radius of forty miles. All the cotton in surrounding counties was shipped from Hampton over the Central to its destination.

The depot at Hampton was then in the center of the town and opposite the building now occupied by The First National Bank. The first agent was Mr. Bill Adair.

Hotels sprang up after the building of the railroad and the first one was owned by John Turnipseed and Ben Thompson, and was under the management of Ben Thompson. Another hotel of that time was the McIntosh Hotel.

The houses of worship, in order of their establishment, were: First—the Primitive Baptist, the Protestant Methodist, the Christian Church, and the Baptist Church. These churches are all represented today in the town, except that the Methodist Episcopal has taken the place of the Protestant Methodist. The Christian Church is a monument to the memory of "Uncle Buck Fears," who built it and who was its pastor for years. Besides these Hampton has four negro churches.

In 1875 occurred the greatest financial boom that Hampton has known. This was the year that George Schaeffer, sent down by Atlanta cotton buyers, was stationed at Hampton; and it was no uncommon sight to see hundreds of wagons of cotton standing in the road along the railroad waiting to be disposed of and then sent down the road for other interests.

Situated in the midst of the richest cotton section it was but natural that manufacturing industries should spring up, and on May 17, 1900, the Hampton Cotton Mills were incorporated. Mr. A. J. Henderson, a wide-awake and energetic citizen started the company that grew and prospered and which at his death, three years ago, was one of the most solid business institutions of its kind in the state. The original capital $50,000.00 and the following directors were elected: President, A. J. Henderson; Vice President, W. P. Wilson; Secretary and Treasurer, W. M. Harris; R. J. Arnold, H. G. Fields, J. L. Moore, and R. F. Smith.

Other original stockholders were P. W. Pullin, J. T. Lewis, and Mrs. Thomas McMahon. In 1904 the capital stock was increased to $100,000.00 and in 1908 was again increased to $150,000.00. In 1917 A. J. Henderson resigned and W. M. Harris was elected president and R. M. Harris, secretary and treasurer. In 1919 its capital stock was increased to $300,000.00 and the plant of Henderson Manufacturing Company was bought. In January, 1920, R. 0. Arnold was elected a director with office of secretary and treasurer and R. M. Harris elected superintendent and general manager. In July, 1920. W. M. Harris resigned as president and R. 0. Arnold was elected president. The present officers and directors are, R. O. Arnold, President; W. P. Wilson, Vice President; R. M. Halo-is, Superintendent and General Manager; W. M. Harris, Chairman Board of Directors; J. L. Moore, H. O. Fields, J. M. Tarpley, and C. V. Williams.

The Hampton Cotton Mills has 1,400 spindles and 41 knitting machines, and 25 sewing machines. They manufacture soft and hard yarns and ladies' underwear. Also operate an ice plant with a capacity of five tons daily. The mills consume about seven or eight thousand bales of cotton annually and employ about two hundred and fifty people.

Besides the mills, Hampton has other industries that are growing. One is a Foundry, which is "owned and operated by Messrs. Arthur and Jim Henderson, both sons of the late A. J. Henderson. The Hampton Milling Company makes both plain and self-rising flour and also has a bleachery for patent flour. In this same plant is a corn mill which is run by electricity.

The Planters Warehouse and Gin Company also ran a grist mill. The Fertilizer Plant, or the Porter Fertilizer Works have a capacity of fifteen thousand tons per year.

The light and water system of Hampton is of the very best. The two deep wells furnish the water supply of Hampton; and it is given up by insurance companies that Hampton has the best water and fire equipment of any town.

The two banks are. The Bank of Hampton and The First National Bank.

The Bank of Hampton was organized and opened for business October 1, 1902, with a paid in capital of $25,000.00. The following were the incorporators: A. J. Henderson, Dr. R. J. Arnold, W. P. Wilson, Smith H. Griffin, W. M. Harris, J. C. Tarpley, W. D. Henderson, J. L. Moore, and I. D. Crawford. The first officers of the bank were, W. P. Wilson, President; Smith H. Griffin, Vice President; J. O. Norris, Cashier. Since the organization, the bank has paid out in cash dividends to the stockholders $57,000.00. The book value of the stock is at the present more than $300.00 per share.

There are few banks in Georgia that have done better than The Bank of Hampton. In fact, it is considered by leading bankers, business men, and state officials as one of the best all-round banks in the State of Georgia. It has always been the policy of the bank to be conservative, yet liberal in its dealings so long as consistent with sound banking. There is no bank that appreciates its good customers more than The Bank of Hampton.

The following are the present officers and directors of the bank: W. P. Wilson, President; David J. Arnold, Vice President; J. O. Rutherford, Cashier; Miss A. L. Rutherford, Assistant Cashier. Directors: W. P. Wilson, David J. Arnold, J. M. Tarpley, J. O. Rutherford, H. G. Fields, H. T. Moore, and J. L. Moore.

The First National Bank of whom W. M. Harris-is President opened for business on November 14, 1911, with a paid in capital of $30,000.00; surplus $3,000.00. The first officers were: President. W. M. Harris; Vice President, A. M. Henderson and E. R. Harris, Cashier. The directors were: W. M. Harris, A, M. Henderson, E. R. Harris, R. E. Henderson, R. M. Harris, W. W. Carmichael, and T. G. Barfield. The present capital is $50,000.00; surplus and undivided profits $40,000.00. As stated W. M. Harris is the President, T. G. Barfield. the Vice President, and E. R. Harris, Cashier. Directors of this bank are: W. M. Harris, R. E. Henderson, R. M. Harris, H. M. Lovern, T. E. Lindler, R. O. Tarpley, and John B. Weldon.

One of the best schools for any town of its size in the state, is the Hampton Public School. Mrs. Lucy P. Richard, who was for ten years connected with the

Georgia Military College, has proven an able and efficient principal for the past three years, and through her suggestion and the efforts of the town at large, it is hoped that September will find the High School enlarged by an additional class. Fostered by the Woman's Club the campus has been beautified and playground equipment procured and the building and grounds are a source of pride to every resident of the town.

Although not every farmer in Hampton is a merchant, yet most every merchant is a farmer. The oldest merchant - though not the oldest man-in Hampton, is J. C. Tarpley. Next in service as a merchant is Hamp Moore. These two have been in business on Main Street in the town for over twenty-five years.

Two of the most modern drug stores in the county are: Cain's Pharmacy and The Service Drug Store.

One of the most up-to-date stores in Hampton is that of H. T. Moore & Company, which is owned and operated by H. T. Moore and "The Moore Boys," Messrs. Arnold, Frank, and Norman Moore. This business house occupies two street fronts and is equipped with style and furnishings with a view to both beauty and service.

Among the other merchants of Hampton are: H. M. Lovern, D. G. Hawkins, W. A. North, The Crescent Mercantile Company owned by Messrs. Moore and Peeples, The Hampton Hardware and Furniture Company owned by L. J. and E. C. Copeland, Henry Hand, and J. L. Turnipseed. The latter is the son of John W. Turnipseed, a pioneer of Hampton.

Some of the prettiest homes in Henry County are those in and around Hampton. Among these may be mentioned the homes of J. L. Moore, A. B. Mitcham, W. M. Harris, Roy Harris, Will Art Wilson, Mrs. Irene Henderson, W. P. Wilson, Henry Moore, Will Edwards, Rome Moore, Robert Peeples, and Jim Minter. Two old homesteads are: The Edward's home, which is west of Hampton and the property of Lemmie Edwards; and "Oaklea," the home of Charles H. Griffin and which was built by his father, Smith H. Griffin. "Oaklea" is east of Hampton on the "Middle McDonough road," and was the scene of many a run-away marriage during the lifetime of Rev. S. H. Griffin.

Hampton District is possessed of unlimited, undeveloped water power. It all has lain in reserve except that which the Georgia Railway and Power Company get from the Towaliga River that heads two miles of Hampton. As yet we only dream of the possibilities contained in the streams that flow between the emerald banks.

It has been said that "History is a drama enacted upon the theater of time," and indeed it is. From the first characters, from the first mayor who presided in the early, days of Bear Creek up to now when our mayor, Mr. J. L. Pritchett, and his efficient Council play their parts in the story of our town, our history has been an unbroken, uninterrupted story with characters and acts befitting the drama which is constantly becoming bigger, better and quicker of action. It is the hope of every Hamptonian, that as the years glide by they, too, may leave works that will make the history of the next hundred years as full of benefit and promise as did the faithful ones whose work they now carry on.

By Miss Emily Griffin
1921

History of Stockbridge

The brevity of this historical record of Stockbridge, gives witness to the undeveloped nature of this portion of Henry County between 1821 - 1921. The writer shares his prophecy for the future of Stockbridge in his statement, *"The town looks out into the future with good prospects of prosperous growth and a useful career among the progressive towns of old Henry County."* A contemporary perspective of the day, as she takes part in the celebration of the county's 100th birthday. Today this account offers a unique perspective into the growth which has taken place since the *History of Stockbridge* was written.

By Reverend W. O. Butler

Among the early settlers of this part of Henry County were the followings; James Coker, Matthew Johnson, Jethro Harrell, Josiah McCulley, Gaston Hinton, Henry Merritt, Dr. Falls, John W. Henderson, James Wllkerson, James Nix, Elijah B. Arnold, Peter Zachry Ward, Davy James, W. W. Bay, 0. McLendon, William Tuggle, Bins Willingham, Wiley Milam, and Joseph Askew.

The town of Stockbridge takes its name from Professor Stockbridge, who taught school at what is now known as Old Stockbridge, before the war of the sixties. Grouped around that place were several houses, among them four log cabins, occupied by Sam Skelton, Lewis Coleman, Mrs. Harriet Brannan, and John Friddle. One of the settlers was Mike Jones, who owned forty acres of land. This property was bought by J. T. Bond, who set up a store, shoe shop, and postoffice. He was also mail carrier, going to and from Jonesboro twice a week on horseback. Another postoffice, called Cotton Indian, Was located three or four miles to the south. Which supplied the people there with mail once a week from Decatur. The first physicians were Dr. Hambrick and Dr. Hightower.

The coming of the Southern Railroad in the year 1881 was an epoch and made great changes. This road was being built from Macon to Atlanta. The settlers who owned land about Old Stockbridge advanced the price of land to such a degree that the people would not buy it. The railroad would not locate a depot there. Two prominent Atlanta citizens, John W. Grant and George W. Adair, came and bought a tract about a mile to the south and offered lots at a reasonable price. This offer was readily accepted by many and on this tract the town of Stockbridge began its existence in 1882.

Before the war of the sixties a settler named William Askew lived in a log cabin on the ground where the town is now built. His widow, Mrs. Emma Askew, still lives there. The first home erected in Stockbridge was built by J. T. Bond, early in 1882, the dwelling in which he now (1921) lives, in his 89th year, its oldest inhabitant. There seems to be some question as to who built the first dwelling in Stockbridge. W. W. Ward is said to be the builder of the first house, and J. T. Bond is given the same honor, so we will say that the two men who built the first two houses were these two citizens.

The first ginnery was put up by Wiley Milam and James Hill about where J. C. Walden's residence now stands. The first- store house was built by J. T. Bond, where the postoffice was kept. John and Dave Suttles also built a store house, followed by J. W. Clark, Sr. The first drug store was established by Dr. Richard Hightower. Among the early merchants were John W.

Grant, J. C. Walden, H. S. Elliott, John and Arthur Mays.

The Masonic Lodge was transferred to Stockbridge in 1890. Its organization dates back to October, 1851, under a warrant issued by the officers of the Grand Lodge of Georgia: William C. Dawson, Grand Master; to E. B. Arnold, T. S. Mays, and S. B. Crawford, of Henry County, being organized at McLendon's store, and called Harmony Lodge, No. 166.

Stockbridge today has about 400 inhabitants, five churches - two of them colored, two schools, a splendid bank, telephone exchange, steam ginnery, eight stores, electric light plants, two cotton warehouses, hotel,, lumber yard, two garages, a commodious brick school building, with auditorium and five recitation rooms; two physicians, one lawyer, and one of the best police officers in the state.

The town is well governed, the present board is composed as follows: W. W. Milam, Sr., mayor; John C. Walden, recorder; J. D. McCullough, clerk, C. M. Power, Joseph Mann, H. M. Askew, C. A. Pless, councilmen, and Vess Moseley, marshal.

The three white churches are in growing condition, having each a good Sunday school and beloved pastors. The Methodist Church, South, pastor is Rev. G. T. Sorrells; the Baptist pastor is Rev. B. W. Collier, of Atlanta, and the Presbyterian pastor is Rev. Mark Hollingsworth, of Hapeville.

The town looks out into the future with good prospects of prosperous growth and a useful career among the progressive towns of old Henry County.

James Coker was a member of the Georgia legislature before railroad days. He rode horseback from Henry County to Milledgeville in order to serve his county as representative.

Elijah B. Arnold later served as representative in the legislature. He was a staunch Union man, and when he saw that Georgia was going into secession, he resigned his seat at Milledgeville and went home.

Some people here remember the time when the only two houses in this section was that one that stood on the spot where the cemetery is located and the other stood near the overhead railroad bridge.

The first painted house in the Stockbridge region was that of James Coker, which stood on the ground now known as the new cemetery.

In 1881 Mayor-William W. Milam, then a ten-year-old boy, saw the laying of the cross-ties and rails of the railroad as it was built to Old Stockbridge.

The first peach orchard set out in the county was by Jethro Harrell, on the ground now known as the new cemetery.

By Rev. W. O. Butler
1921

History of Women's Clubs of Henry County

This thorough historical record of the *Women's Clubs of Henry County,* illustrates the dedication to community service, care and respect for those in need and the organization's sincere purpose to make a positive impact. Their example is nothing less than inspirational. The statements of introduction below, which outline the beliefs, focus and purpose, are today as valid a template for good citizenship, as they were in 1921. Indeed this portion of the Henry County 100th birthday celebration of 1921, was not only a record of accomplishment but also a record of the identity of those that lived.

By Mrs. E. M. Copeland

Women have been organizing themselves into clubs for the general purpose of receiving mutual counsel and helpfulness and that their united influence and service might promote educational, civic, social, and moral advancement in the community, county, and state. They have felt that they must establish new and better purpose in life; must believe in and practice sincerity to each other, kindness to all with whom they come in contact, in generous love and strong friendship. They must seek the good in every person, and with charity, truth, and reverence as keywords to life's cipher, must develop to its highest power every capability of mind, soul, and body.

Then with incontrovertible faith in beautiful and harmonious law and the ultimate triumph of the Divine in man must consecrate themselves anew to the service of God and humanity.

There are now more than 40,000 women in Georgia who have pledged themselves to greater and nobler service.

Every true woman wears the badge of service from that of home to that of public good. The club - women are called the unpaid servants of humanity. They are making every effort: to practice thrift as requested by the government.

They are urging state censorship for movies to secure better and cleaner pictures.

Modern dress and the modern ways of the youth of today have been protested against.

Club women are thoroughly interested in every phase of education. It has been said that "man has more faith in life as a teacher - the woman more faith in schools," and she has given ample proof of this faith in sponsoring rural schools, in organizing school improvement clubs in rural districts, cooperating with school authorities in obliterating illiteracy, securing consolidation of schools, and in library work. They have provided a student loan fund for the benefit of girls who are unable to secure educational advantages. About 170 girls have been aided through this Student Loan Fund. They may attend any school in the United States and while most have attended our various Georgia schools many have gone to Columbia, Vanderbilt, Chicago University, and Vassar. They are maintaining a real mission school at Tallulah Falls for the benefit of the mountain children. These children board in the school and are taught in the literary department and also industrial arts. Many wonderful and gratifying results have come from this school, particularly one mountain girl has shown such genius in the industrial arts that she has become a teacher in the institution and has had her expenses paid for special training in New York for the past two summers.

Last year we advocated some law by which mothers with young babies could receive instruction and care. On December 6th following, the Sheppard-Towner bill was introduced in congress and it is receiving the earnest support of club women all over the states. It will provide just the help for which we asked, but as yet Georgia has made no provision for pensioning widows with dependent children. Many clubs have been instrumental in having medical inspection placed in the schools.

Citizenship is uppermost in the minds of the new citizens at present and especially the two phases which must receive immediate attention. First, Registration. No time must be lost in conforming to the latter of the law by registering. Second, Preparation for Citizenship. Study citizenship, know its methods. Let the motto be, "Every club a training camp for citizenship."

Our question today is not whether we want suffrage or not but how are we going to use it? The power has been placed upon us and the club women are going to meet the issue squarely and prepare themselves for their responsibilities. Instead of pleading for what women want, the women can simply decide what they want and secure the promise before the vote in cast for the candidate. The policy of the federation has always been and will continue to be "measures not men, policies not party," but let it be also known, there are 7,000 more women in Georgia than men. We will see that women are not going into their new power to seek to wrest from men the reins of government nor to be their rivals in places of power. It will be the privilege of woman to be in the affairs of state. as she has been in those of the home, his helpmeet, and together they will solve the problems that confront them and together work to make the world a better place to live in.

Henry County Federation

The Henry County Federation of Women's Clubs was organized in February, 1917, for the purpose of stimulating club work in Henry County by mutual counsel and co-operation.

The co-operative spirit of the clubs is gratifying and helpful. The definite work now planned is that each club shall endeavor to organize one School Improvement Club during each year until every community shall have been reached, thus securing better schools, school facilities and general community improvement in towns and outlying districts. We are glad to report that Hampton, through Miss Emily Griffin, has organized such a club near them and is planning to organize a School Improvement Club for their school. The other clubs are making similar efforts in this direction.

County exchange library system has also been planned, beginning in clubs already organized, and extending to others as they shall be organized, hoping by this movement to lay foundation for a County Circulating Library.

Mrs. John Brown, of Locust Grove, was first president; Mrs. Rosser Ward, of Stockbridge, succeeding her. The office at present is 4eld by Mrs. E.

M. Copeland, of McDonough, with Mrs. R. H. Daniel, secretary and treasurer.

The county presidents have visited the clubs and have found splendid enthusiastic organizations with capable, efficient leaders, who have proven themselves a tower of strength to the Federation. Three county conventions have been held with distinguished club women addressing the assemblies, among whom were the late lamented Mrs. Nellie Peters Black, then president of the Georgia Federation; Mrs. Samuel Lumpkin, national chairman of Thrift; Miss Templeton of Library commission, and Mrs. Alonzo Richardson, state chairman of Citizenship.

The Federation through a petition to County Road Commissioner, helped to secure a splendid highway between McDonough and Locust Grove, also asked officials to remove old carpet from the court house stairway and remove other objectionable features to which request they courteously complied. Federation made donation of $100.00 to Tallulah Falls School.

The representatives of the Federation met with the teachers at their County Institute in December, 1920, and tendered to them co-operation in every possible way and in turn the teachers pledged co-operation in the school improvement work which was very gratifying, as this work must be accomplished jointly in a sympathetic understanding way. At this meeting the Federation served a delicious luncheon to the teachers and the two parted in hearty good will.

The Federation is designed to be a real power in club work and we feel that it is beginning to fulfill its object.

Women's Club of Stockbridge

We will begin by paying tribute to the mother of all club life in Stockbridge, Mrs. Harriet Tucker Hawkins, feeling the need of something worth while and uplifting for her community, conceived the idea of forming a study class known as the Mildred Rutherford Historical Circle.

In 1916 Mrs. R. H. Hankinson, president of the Sixth District Federation, addressed the Circle on importance of joining the State Federation which they decided to do, becoming Stockbridge Woman's Club. First meeting was held at home of Mrs. Augustus Swann where constitution and by-laws were adopted and officers elected, Mrs. Edward Austin being first president, Mrs. Augustus Swann following and Mrs. Rosser Ward now holding that office.

The charter members were, Mrs. S. C. McWilliams, Mrs. R. H. Hankinson, Mrs. Harriet Hawkins, Mrs. Ed Austin, Mrs. Augustus Swann, Miss Ward McWilliams, and Mrs. Berry Hinton.

Miss Ward McWilliams represented the club at state convention held in Macon in October, 1916. Mrs. Augustus Swann and Mrs. Rosser Ward represented the club at Griffin, May 22. 1918, at district convention.

The first work undertaken was beautifying the school grounds by planting pecan trees and making other improvements which the club continues to do from year to year. In 1917 a civic committee was appointed which immediately formulated plans for clean-up-week, this custom has been strictly adhered to since.

In response to patriotic call the club invested in war savings stamps and Liberty bonds, and sent a box to Belgian sufferers. Later Red Cross work was taken up at which members labored untiringly, also sending boxes of jellies and delicacies' to the hospital at Fort McPherson.

Twenty dollars was contributed to Red Cross and a war orphan was adopted by club. The club also contributed to the purchase of a piano for school. Regular contributions have been made to Tallulah Falls School, Student Aid Fund, and Ella F. White Memorial.

Mrs. Augustus Swann and Mrs. Bessie Ward were representatives to district convention in Macon in May, 1919. Mrs. Rosser Ward attended district convention at Round Oak, and also was delegate to state convention in Atlanta in 1920.

The club entertained the County Federation at home of Mrs. S. C. McWilliams April 21, 1920. Mrs. Samuel Lumpkin and Miss Charlotte Templeton being among the distinguished guests. The club entertained the chamber of commerce with officials of Radcliffe Chautauqua at a luncheon hoping to create interest in the chautauqua movement to be given under auspices of Woman's Club.

To stimulate interest in club work visitors from other clubs were invited to meet with them. The club joined with the County Federation in giving a luncheon to the teachers of the County Institute at their December meeting in McDonough, thus stimulating interest along educational lines and pledging co-operation with the teachers and trustees of our schools. Nineteen members are enrolled at present.

Hampton Civic League

The Hampton Civic League was organized in 1915 by Miss Celeste Parish for the purpose of interesting the women in the upbuilding of their school. It was federated later.

Since that time the Club has been one of the most active organizations of the town under the leadership of the following presidents: Mrs. C. N. Fields, Mrs. Tyman Bowden, Mrs. Rome Moore, and Mrs. Grady Fears. It has always stood for the highest civic interests of the community as well as for the highest good of home, school, and children. It has grown steadily in numbers and influence and has accomplished much that is valuable to the town.

During the war club members did active and effective war work, Red Cross activities, and sent many delicacies to soldiers at Fort McPherson. Supported a French orphan during the war and co-operated with the government in all of its requests to bring peace as quickly as possible.

To Near East Relief it has contributed $20,00. has provided medicine and clothing for a needy family, and furnished one picnic dinner for the convicts; also makes yearly donations to Tallulah Falls School.

Much time and effort have been devoted to educational work lectures and lyceum numbers of the club. Special interest has been taken in the upkeep and beautifying of public school building and play ground. A library, book cases, a lavatory, and other necessities have been installed in school building. School grounds have been improved by cement walks, flowers, hedges, and play ground equipment.

A club of county women has been organized and fostered, also a troop of girl scouts is being sponsored by the club, and club is co-operating with county chairman of registration.

On the 22nd of April the club entertained the County Federation at the home of Mrs. J. O. Turner. This meeting was of great interest and Mrs. Alonzo Richardson charmed the assembly with her delightful manner and the very practical message which she delivered on Citizenship.

Locust Grove Woman's Club

The Locust Grove Civic League was organized in 1913 as a result of a union prayer meeting of the Methodist and Baptist Missionary Societies for the purpose of civic improvement.

In 1914 quite an interesting event was the first "clean up" day when all the members turned out in full force, serving a delightful basket luncheon at the noon hour. During the rest hour the mayor and pastors of the churches made short addresses commending the splendid public spirit of the club, and always since this time the organization has met with the heartiest co-operation of the men of the town, who realize that the club stands for the highest good of the community.

Mrs. Claude Gray was first president and served until the civic league federated in 1917, when its name was changed to Locust Grove Woman's Club. Mrs. John Gardner became president and has been succeeded by Mrs. John S. Brown who now fills that office.

The club fulfilled its patriotic duties during the great war by entering into all of the activities to which the women were called, and the record made will ever be a matter of pride because of the devotion and sacrifices so freely offered in the cause of liberty to-secure the safety of the' world.

The club each year donates $5.00 each to cleaning of public buildings and parks. Hedges have been planted around the school grounds and trees are planted where needed.

Flowers also have been planted to beautify many barren spots and seats have been placed in parks for the comfort of the public, also swings for the pleasure of the children.

Arbor Day was observed this year. Quite a number of trees were planted and an appropriate program was rendered by pupils of the Gramman School. The club donated $75.00 for this work.

The club contributed regularly to Tallulah Falls School.

The social service committee visits the sick and cheers them with gifts of flowers.

Means of raising funds for civic improvements are many and varied - mostly by entertainments consisting of programs. A George Washington party netted quite a neat sum. Yearly a Halloween party is given -which is the largest social affair. The whole town is invited and the largest building of the town is secured to accommodate the merry makers.

The usual Halloween games are played and many things are sold from the gaily decorated booths. This entertainment nets about $100.00.

Many books have been bought each year and donated both to Grammar School and Locust Grove Institute. Through this means and other ways the Institute has acquired quite a nice library which is used by the town at large.

This club has a membership of sixty-two loyal and willing workers whose past achievements are but the promise of a fuller and brighter future - when the women, who have come into their own, will be a great uplifting force in every phase of community, county, and state life.

McDonough Woman's Club

McDonough Woman's Club was organized through special efforts of Mrs. Paul Turner, at her home, April 18, 1916. Mrs. Bruce Jones, of Macon, the president of Sixth District Federation of Clubs, presided at this meeting and also federated the club at that time. There were thirty-eight charter members, and Mrs. R. H. Hankinson was first president. Later she was succeeded by Mrs. E. M. Copeland. Mrs. Adam Sloan now holds the office.

The first and possibly most important work done by the club was founding a library. Beginning with a few volumes donated by club members and interested friends, it has grown through the years by donation and purchase until 1,300 volumes have been accumulated. Homeless at the beginning it was provided for at various times by courtesy of Copeland-Turner Mere Co., First National Bank, and T. A. Sloan & Co. Outgrowing its quarters from time to time necessitated many moves. At last more commodious quarters were offered by the County in its splendid court house, which the club gladly accepted, feeling now that a permanent home had been procured. Some spacious rooms have been fitted up in the basement - beautifully cleaned, calcimined, shelved, and painted - providing not only library space but a room for county club meetings and a much needed rest room for the visiting ladies from other parts of the county. The rest room has been made comfortable by some furnishings done by the club but much more will be done in the near future.

A beautiful and substantial wall has been built about the park at the instigation of the club, part of the funds being raised by the club.

County and club working in co-operation have made this the greatest civic improvement of the town.

Flowers have been planted about the court house and seed have been supplied by club for planting city park, which adds much to the appearance of the town, also civic pride has been stimulated by public clean-up days.

Through club efforts a curtain for stage in the school auditorium was secured and material for decorating the stage was donated at one time.

The club has the honor of fostering the Red Cross movement in McDonough, securing its organization through earnest and patriotic effort. The club women during the war period gave themselves entirely to war work, not alone to Red Cross, but to Belgian relief and conservation - holding two canning and substitute food demonstrations. Also at the government's request making house to house canvas to get food conservation cards signed and selling Liberty bonds, and Thrift Stamps. In fact, co-operating in every possible way to bring victory to American arms and thereby peace to a war-torn and broken- hearted world.

Of the $1,448.00 raised by the club in the past five years, contributions have been made to the State Federation causes - Tallulah Falls School and Student Aid Fund.

A war orphan was supported during the war period and a substantial contribution was made to Near East Relief Fund.

Over $400.00 in bonds and thrift stamps have been set apart as pledge to the Memorial fund, which cause has been temporarily suspended because of stringency of the times.

During these years regular study courses have been carried on - Parliamentary Law, History of Georgia, History of the Great War and Its Outstanding Figures, and latterly, Citizenship in Many of Its Phases.

Many distinguished club women have been guests and have delivered addresses before the body, among whom were Mrs. R. L. Berner, of Macon; Mrs. Nellie Peters Black, of Atlanta; Mrs. J. E. Hayes, of Montezurna, president of Georgia Federation; Mrs. Hugh Wellett, of Atlanta, director of Tallulah Falls School, and Mrs. Samuel Inman, State Director of National Federation Club entertained the Sixth District Federation in May, 1917, at the Presbyterian Church. Many state officers were present and club members had opportunity to meet and hear these veterans of club service, gaining both information and inspiration.

By Mrs. E. M. Copeland

1921

The Methodist
Circuit Riding Preacher

CIRCUIT- RIDERS

The father of Methodism, John Wesley's plan of multiple meeting places called circuits required an itinerating force of preachers. A circuit was made up of two or more local churches (sometimes referred to as societies) in early Methodism. In American

Methodism circuits were sometimes referred to as a "charge." A pastor would be appointed to the charge by his bishop. During the course of a year he was expected to visit each church on the charge at least once, and possibly start some new ones. At the end of a year the pastors met with the bishop at annual conference, where they would often be appointed to new charges. A charge containing only one church was called a station. The traveling preachers responsible for caring for these societies, or local churches and stations, became known as circuit-riders, or sometimes saddlebag preachers. As illustrated in the early 19th century engraving above, they traveled light, carrying their belongings and books in their saddlebags. Ranging far and wide through villages and wilderness, they preached daily or more often at any site available be it a log cabin, the local court house, a meeting house, or an outdoor forest setting. Unlike the pastors of settled denominations, these itinerating preachers were constantly on the move. Their assignment was often so large it might take them 5 or 6 weeks to cover the territory. The Methodist saddlebag preachers, like cowboys, were wholly committed to their horses. It was no wonder because the nineteenth-century preacher, either by saddle horse or carriage, had no other way to reach the people. At Conference, after appointments were made, there would often be a great time of horse trading among the preachers.

Those who were assigned to distant circuits would trade horses with those who were going to towns or villages where stronger horses would not be needed. The horse was appreciated.

Henry County in the Civil War

Henry county suffered greatly in the war. While the "Gone With The Wind" movie is fictional, the story line closely follows what we know of the families who went through the war from Henry County.

Seven companies were formed from Henry County. This volume contains the roster of four of these, the 19th, Co. G, the 22nd, Co. K, and the 44th Companies A and I.

Companies formed in whole or in part from Henry County:

GA 19th Infantry Regiment, Company G

GA 22nd Infantry Regiment, Company K

GA 27th Infantry Regiment, Company H

GA 30th Infantry Regiment, Company E

GA 44th Infantry Regiment, Company A

GA 44th Infantry Regiment, Company I

GA 53rd Infantry Regiment, Company F

The Georgia 19th Infantry Regiment Company G

This company appears to have been organized as Co. G, 2d Regiment, 4th Brigade, Georgia State Troops June 11, 1861. There is only one roll of this company on file in the War Department, Washington, D. C., and it is apparently only a roster of men who tendered their services to the President of the Confederate States; hence there are some conflicts in dates of elections and promotions.

First Hand Account By Silas Oglesby

Company G.

[REF: http://www.fred.net/stevent/19GA/oglesby.html]

In the summer of 1861 Company G 19th Georgia Henry Guard with Capt. T.W. Flynt in charge was organized at Shingleroof camp ground (near McDonough, GA) from there to Big Shanty was organized into a Regiment with Col. Boyd as commander.

We set off to Lynchburg in early fall then to Manassas we remained at Manassas until April of 1862. We came with in 18 miles of Richmond, there I took the measles and was in the rain for 2 days. We walked 9 miles in the rain and spent the night in a house vacated by refugees. Next day we finished the tramp to Richmond reaching there during the night and slept in a car shed after I recovered I had a relapse and was very sick I stayed their 2 more weeks

Later I was sent to Lynchburg to a Hospital and found some kin folks was very sick but left the hospital to stay with them and did so until July. Started back to my command just after the Seven

Days Battle" "Tough Friday slept in a RR cut Saturday went on pickett duty in woods. At 3:00 PM was driven back by Federals to the RR cut but we managed to drive them back into the woods. Soon my brigade, which was at the extreme left charged a federal battery and captured the same all the federals retreated. I had been struck twice my scabbard turning one and a tin plate in my knape sack turning the other. Not hurt much"

8/30/1862 "Went to field hospital and stayed there 9 days had one piece of bread to eat, and mostly lived on green apples and green corn. Left there and overtook army at Fredricksburg City, Maryland was there a few days.

We then recrossed the Potomac and went to Harpers Ferry and captured same. Went back up the river and recrossed and was at the Battle of Sharpesburg where my brother in law Gus Owens was critically wounded and later died."

"We then went into camp at Bunker Hill. In November we crossed the Blue Ridge and went to Fredricksburg on December 13. Had a big fight and was wounded in the hip and captured on that day. December 25, 1862, was carried to Washington DC and put in a Yankee hospital and had wound treated for the first time. Only two confederates including myself the other died soon after my arrival.

Was moved to the Old Capitol Prison the latter part of April 1863 five days later I was exchanged and sent to Petersburg, VA and got furlough home in the first part of May. Went home and stayed until August in the mean time my regiment had been transferred to Colquitts Georgia Brigade and had been sent to Charleston, SC."

I joined them there in August and stayed on James Island until the end of March 1864 then left for Florida. Had a fight at Ocean Pond and we whipped the Yankees Bad, drove them back to Jacksonville. I was hit in the back but not hurt to bad. It was a rich battle field got lots of money, blankets, watches ect. We stayed near Jacksonville for a while then returned to Virginia"
"We got to Petersburg and found yanks on RR between Richmond and Petersburg and had a hard fight but drove them off. Next we fought at Druids Bluff with Burnside went from there to Richmond and from there to Cold Harbor and had several fights.

Yanks moved across the James River to Petersburg 6/17/1864 we reached Petersburg. Yanks had captured Fort Stedman our works at the time so we threw up new works on the night of the 17th. On the 18th they messed troops on us at Hairs Hill and charged us with 11 lines but were repulsed by us, we lost few while they lost hundreds."

"I had a younger brother George H. Tobie killed at the beginning of the Battle of Petersburg I saw the explosion.   In the fall of 1864 George Walker and myself captured 500 yankee prisoners on the Weldon or SS Railroad. We them returned to Richmond and charged Fort Harrison but were repulsed after a hard fight we fell back across the river."

"We stayed at Laurel Hill Church until 12/25/1864 then left for Wilmington, NC then to Kingston and then on to Bentonville where colonel Neal was killed in battle but we managed to hold out against Sherman's Army. We went near Raleigh about 30 miles and camped. About the first of April 1865 we marched and and came within one day of Raleigh. The next day we marched threw and learned that Gen. Lee had surrendered but we continued our march to Greensboro their surrendering to Sherman.

Sixty of our men were furnished with wagons and supplies and we marched on foot to Athens, GA from there we took a train to Conyers and from there I walked home alone to McDonough on foot."

Flynt, Tilghman W.- Captain July 2, 1861. Wounded, leg dis- abled at Sharpsburg, Md., September 17, 1862. Elected Lieutenant Colonel August 20, 1863. Retired to Invalid Corps September 17, 1864. Resigned in 1864. (Born in Georgia February 24,1827.)

Stokes, Henry-1st Lieutenant July 2,1861. Resigned, disability, September 1,1862.

Selfridge, John R.-2d Lieutenant July 2,1861. Elected 1st Lieutenant September 1, 1862. Wounded at Fredericksburg, Va. December 13, 1862. Died of wounds in General Hospital #16, at Richmond, Va., February 19,1863.

Elliott, Baylor S.-Jr. 2d Lieutenant July 2, 1861. Elected 2d Lieutenant September 1, 1862; 1st Lieutenant February 17, 1863; Captain August 20,1863. Killed at Weldon Railroad, Va. August 19,1864.

Wise, George E.-1st Sergeant July 2,1861. Elected Lieutenant.

Elliott, John R.-2d Sergeant July 2,1861. Elected Jr. 2d Lieu- tenant September 1,1862; Captain August 20,1864. No later record.

Speer, James H.-3d Sergeant July 2,1861. No later record.

Phillips, James R.-4th Sergeant July 2,1861. Paid for commutation of rations while on furlough from August 10, to September 18, 1863, at James Island, S. C. November 28,1863.

Love, Mark J.-5th Sergeant July 2, 1861. Appointed 1st Ser- geant September 1, 1862. Elected Jr. 2d Lieutenant October 2, 1862. Wounded in left leg at Fredericksburg, Va. December 13, 1862. No later record. (Resident of Georgia since March 1858.)

Maddox, John D.-1st Corporal July 2,1861. No later record.

Moseley, John W.- 2d Corporal July 2, 1861. Died of typhoid fever in Chimborazo Hospital #4, at Richmond, Va. August 15, 1862.

Elliott, George, T.-3d Corporal July 2, 1861. On sick furlough for 30 days from February 16,1862. Appointed Sergeant. Died April 7,1863.

Owens, Augustus-4th Corporal July 2,1861. Appointed 4th Ser- geant July 1862. Wounded and captured at Sharpsburg, Md. September 17, 1862. Paroled September 30, 1862. Admitted to U. S. A.

General Hospital #5, at Frederick, Md. October 15, 1862, where left thigh was amputated October 1862. Died October 28,1862.

Privates:

Alexander, Henry S.- private July 2,1861. Appointed Corporal. Wounded at Cold Harbor, Va. June 27, 1862; Sharpsburg, Md. September 17,1862. Killed at Petersburg, Va. January 1865.

Allums, John- private July 2, 1861. Wounded June 1863. Died of wounds.

Allums, William Jefferson- private July 2, 1861. Wounded in leg, necessitating amputation, at 2d Manassas, Va. August 30,1862. Received pay at Macon, Ga. July 18,1864. No later record.

Amos, Rufus L.- private July 2, 1861. Appointed 4th Sergeant September 17,1861. Killed at Mechanicsville, Va. June 26,1862.

Bledsoe, William H.- private July 2, 1861. Died of pneumonia at Camp Johnson, Va. January 27,1862.

Bonner, John - private July 15, 1861. Wounded at Mechanics- ville, Va. June 26, 1862. Captured at Sharpsburg, Md. September 28, 1862. Paroled at Fort McHenry, Md. November 12, 1862. Received at City

Point, Va. for exchange, November 21,1862. No later record.

Boynton, John N.- private July 2, 1861. Killed at Mechanics- ville, Va. June 26,1862.

Brown, Warren J.- private July 2, 1861. Died in Virginia December 10,1861.

Bunn, William- private. Captured August 23, 1864. Transferred to City Point, Va. for exchange February 25,1865. No later record.

Carmichael, John R.- private July 2,1861. No later record.

Carroll, William Anson- private July 2,1861. On detail duty in Army Intelligence Office August 1862 - June 1864. No later rec- ord. (Born in McDonough, Ga. June 22,1837.)

Cole, Clem C.- private July 2,1861. Died of disease in Henry County, Ga. June 13,1863.

Connally, George W.- private July 2,1861. Wounded at Seven Pines, Va. May 30,1862. Appointed 4th Corporal September 17,1863; 3d Sergeant. Surrendered, Greensboro, N. C. April 26,1865.

Cook, Benjamin F.- private July 2,1861. Died in Charlottes- ville, Va. hospital November 27,1861.

Cook, Jabez F.- private July 2,1861. Wounded at Mechanics- ville, Va. June 26,1862. Paid at Richmond, Va. August 2,1862. No later record.

Cook, William N.- private March 1,1862. Died in Richmond, Va. hospital June 11,1862.

Crabbe, George H.- private July 2,1861. Appointed 1st Ser- geant in 1861. Surrendered, Greensboro, N. C. April 26,1865.

Crabbe, William J.- private July 2, 1861. Wounded, leg dis- abled, at Fort Fisher, N. C., January 15,1865. Surrendered, Greens boro, N. C. April 26,1865.(Born in Georgia November 1,1845.)

Elliott, Henry S.- private July 2,1861. Surrendered, Greens- boro, N. C. April 26,1865.

Elliott, Hiram T.- private July 2,1861. Captured at Fredericks- burg, Va. December 13,1862. Paroled for exchange at camp near Fal mouth, Va. December 14, 1862. Wounded at Chancellorsville, Va. December 3,1863. In Jackson Hospital at Richmond, Va. December 31,1864. No later record.

Elliott, John Joseph- private March 3,1862. Died May 29,1862.

Elliott, Septimus Adolphus- private July 2,1861. Died of dis- ease in Brigade Hospital at James Island, S. C. December 22,1863.

Elliott, Thomas S.- private July 2,1861. Wounded at Mechanicsville, Va. June 26,1862. Appointed Subenrolling Officer for Henry County, Ga. June 3,1863, and served as such to close of war. (Born in Georgia in 1838.)

English, John R.- private July 2,1861. Killed at Mechanicsville, Va. June 26,1862.

Farris, Joel H.- private July 2,1861. Died from wounds re- ceived by accidental discharge of gun July 3,1862.

Fisher, James M.- private July 2,1861. No later record.

Gardner, Pitts J.- private July 2,1861. Sick in hospital February 1862. No later record.

Gleaton, George W.(or Gladen)- private July 2,1861. Wounded in leg, necessitating amputation, and captured at Sharpsburg, Md. September 17,1862. Released at Fort McHenry, Md. and sent to Fortress Monroe, Va. for exchange March 13,1863.

Gosden, Frank W - private July 2,1861. No later record.

Gosden, James (or Gosdin)- private July 2,1861.

Gosden, William F.(or Gosdin)- private July 2,1861. Admitted to Jackson Hospital at Richmond, Va., with chronic diarrhoea, October 9, 1864. Returned to duty November 3, 1864. Paroled at General Hospital at Thomasville, N. C. May 1,1865.

Grant, Benjamin W.- private July 2, 1861. Discharged, dis- ability, May 1,1862.

Grant, Isaac A.- private July 2,1861. Died, result of accidental shot received in camp at Richmond, Va., August 14,1862.

Grant, John- private July 2,1861. Discharged, disability, December 1861.

Gray, Jonathan S.- private July 2,1861. Killed at Seven Pines, Va. May 30,1862.

Gray, J. A.- private August 9,1862. Detailed nurse in Staunton, Va. hospital December 1,1862. Died of pneumonia at Staunton, Va. December 21,1862. Buried there in Thornrose Cemetery. Appears on records as of Co. G, and Co. I. The Captain of Co. G, stated no such man was a member of his company, but the Captain of Co. I, stated that a man of that name was assigned to his company.

Gray, Nelson- private July 2,1861. No later record.

Gray, Oliver S.- private July 2,1861. Transferred to Co. A, January 11,1862. No later record.

Guest, James M.- private July 2,1861. Transferred to Co. A, January 11,1862. Captured at Weldon Railroad, Va. August 19,1864. Took oath of allegiance to U. S. Govt. and joined U. S. service at Point Lookout, Md. October 14,1864.

Hambrick, John B.- private July 2,1861. Elected Lieutenant in 1861. Discharged, furnished substitute, July 1862.

Hand, James- private July 2,1861.

Hand, Johnson- private July 2,1861. Died of disease in 1861.

Hand, Thomas H.- private. Admitted to C. S. A. Hospital at Petersburg, Va. May 23,1864; Remarks : "June 6,1864, duty." No later record.

Harper, Henry- private July 2,1861.

Harper, John- private July 2,1861.

Harper, Robert H.- private December 30, 1862. Wounded at Chancel- lorsville, Va. May 3, 1863; Drewry's Bluff, Va. May 16, 1864. In 1st Division General Hospital at Camp Winder, Richmond, Va., June 21,1864. No later record. (Born in Georgia September 17,1844.)

Harper, Thomas- private July 2,1861.

Harper, T. L. (or T. S.)- private 1862. In hospital May 4, 1863 - January 7,1864. No later record.

Hooten, Cosby A.- private July 2, 1861. Died of typhoid fever in General Hospital #18, at Richmond, Va., December 10,1861.

Jackson, Marcus L. C.- private July 2,1861. Appointed Sergeant June 1, 1862. Died of disease at Camp Winder Hospital at Richmond, Va., August 25,1862. Buried there in Hollywood Ceme tery. (Born in Henry County, Ga. in 1834.)

Johnson, George Allen- private July 2, 1861. Died in Richmond, Va. hospital August 1862.

Johnson, James A.- private July 2, 1861. Died near Fredericks- burg, Va. March 12,1862.

Johnson, James M.- private. Admitted to General Hospital at Farmville, Va. August 31, 1862. Returned to duty October 16, 1862. Wounded at Fredericksburg, Va. December 13, 1862. Furloughed for 40 days January 27, 1863. Received pay for commutation of rations at Macon, Ga. August 26, 1863, while on detached duty as Sub enrolling Officer from June 9, 1863. On duty as Sub-enrolling Officer in Clayton County, Ga. from June 9, 1863, to June 10, 1864. No later record.

Johnson, Jesse James- private July 2,1861. Appointed Musician. Pension records show he was furloughed for 30 days in spring of 1865. Captured at Columbus, Ga. in 1865.

Johnson, Luke- private July 2,1861.

Johnson, William R.- private July 2, 1861. Killed at Harper's Ferry, Va. September 12,1862.

Kelley, Henry H. (or Kelly)- private July 2, 1861. Elected 2d Lieutenant February 17, 1863; 1st Lieutenant in 1864. Surrendered, Greensboro, N. C. April 26,1865.

Kelley, John M. (or Kelly)- private July 2, 1861. Admitted to Jackson Hospital at Richmond, Va. December 16, 1864, and died there of chronic diarrhoea, February 5, 1865. Buried there in Hollywood Cemetery.

Kelley, Joseph T. (or Kelly)- private July 2, 1861. Died May 21,1862. Buried in Hollywood Cemetery at Richmond, Va.

Lewis, Lewis- private July 2, 1861. Transferred to Co. A, January 11,1862. Killed at Bentonville, N. C. April 26,1865.

Maddox, Jacob- private July 2, 1861 Admitted to Chimborazo Hospital #3, at Richmond, Va., with pneumonia, April 2, 1862. Furloughed for 60 days June 12, 1862. Discharged, furnished substitute, in 1864.

Maddox, Madison- private July 2, 1861. Wounded in hand in 1862. Admitted to Chimborazo Hospital #3, at Richmond, Va., October 6, 1862. Furloughed for 40 days October 19, 1862. No later record.

Massey, Thomas- private July 2,1861. No later record.

McCord, William H. H.- private July 2, 1861. Appointed Com- missary Sergeant. Surrendered, Greensboro, N. C. April 26, 1865.

McDaniel Simeon C.- private July 2, 1861. Captured at Weldon Railroad, Va. August 19, 1864. Paroled at Elmira, N. Y. March 14, 1865. Received at Boulware &

Cox's Wharves, James River, Va. for exchange, March 18-21,1865. No later record.

Merritt, William Parks- private July 2,1861. Appointed Color Corporal July 1861. Wounded at Cedar Run, Va. August 9,1862.

Mobley, William F.- private July 2,1861. Admitted to General Hospital #9, at Richmond, Va. October 4,1862. Sent to Hospital #17. No later record.

Morris, Darling D.- private July 2, 1861. Left General Hospital at Howard's Grove, Richmond, Va. February 11,1862. Wounded at Ocean Pond, Fla. February 20,1864. Died of wounds, Madison Fla., February 22,1864. Buried there.

Moseley, Josephus- private July 2,1861. Pension records show he surrendered at Greensboro, N. C. April 26,1865. (Born in Henry County, Ga. July 27,1833.)

Moseley, Peter G.- private July 2,1861. Discharged, furnished Wilkinson as substitute, in 1862.

Moseley, William T.- private July 2,1861. Wounded, date and place not given. Admitted to Chimborazo Hospital #3, at Rich mond, Va., with diarrhoea, October 23,1862. Wounded through head and left arm at Kinston, N. C. March 8,1865. Paroled at Charlotte, N. C. May 3,1865. (Born in Georgia February 16,1837.)

Oglesby, George H.(Tobe)- private July 2, 1861. Killed at Petersburg, Va. April 3,1865.

Oglesby, Gus. Name not listed in Henderson's Roster. Enlisted July 2, 1861 at Camp Shingleroof near Big Shanty, GA. Critically wounded at the battle of Sharpsburg and later died.

REF:
http://www.fred.net/stevent/19GA/oglesby.html

Oglesby, Robert L- private July 2,1861. Wounded at battle of Sharpsburg. Died in General Hospi tal at Camp Winder, Richmond, Va. October 10,1862.

Oglesby, Silas Moseley.- private July 2,1861. Appointed Corporal. Wounded at 2d Manassas, Va. August 30,1862. Captured at Fredericksburg, Va. August 30,1862. Exchanged. Surrendered, Greensboro, N. C. April 26,1865. Born 1844, Henry County, GA Died 1891

Owen, William H.- private July 2,1861. Appointed Sergeant. Discharged, disability, February 19,1863.

Phillips, Arrington- private July 2, 1861. Died at Manassas, Va. December 25,1862.

Phillips, Hardy- private July 2,1861.

Phillips, John A.- private July 2, 1861. Died at Warrenton, Va. December 25,1861.

Phillips, John G.- private July 2,1861. Died in General Hospital #9, at Richmond, Va. June 27,1862.

Phillips, Robert B.- private July 2,1861. Discharged on ac- count of chronic rheumatism March 28,1862.

Phillips, W. C.- private July 2,1861. No later record.

Puckett, John A.- private July 2,1861. Captured at Weldon Railroad, Va. August 19,1864. Released at Point Lookout, Md., on joining U. S. Army, October 14,1864. Enlisted as a private in Co. A,4th Regiment U. S. Vols. October 31,1864, and mustered out June 19,1866. (Born in Newton County, Ga. January 16,1827.)

Rape, Milton A.- private July 2,1861. Discharged, disability, July 25,1861.

Rape, Peter- private July 2,1861. Paid at Richmond, Va. September 29,1862. No later record.

Richards, John R. (or John A.)- private July 2, 1861. Ap- pointed Color Corporal July 1861. Transferred to Co. K, 22d Regiment Ga. Inf. March 1, 1862.

Discharged on account of dropsy at Falling Creek, Va. July 17,1862.

Rowan, Abraham Alex- private July 2,1861. Killed at Mechanics- ville, Va. June 26,1862.

Rowden, Elijah A.- private July 2, 1861. Wounded and cap- tured at Fredericksburg, Va. December 13, 1862. Exchanged near Falmouth, Va. December 14, 1862. Paid at Richmond, Va. August 25, 1864. No later record.

Setzer, John- private July 2, 1861. Wounded at 2d Manassas, Va. August 30, 1862. Surrendered at Greensboro, N. C. April 26, 1865.

Sherrer, James T.- private July 2, 1861. Transferred to Co. I, l3th Regiment Alabama Inf. November 24, 1862. Discharged, disability, at General Hospital, Danville, Va., August 1,1863.

Sims, Cicero H.- private August 1863. Captured at Weldon Rail- road, Va. August 19, 1864. Exchanged February 13, 1865. Pension records show he was at home on furlough close of war. (Born in Franklin County, Ga. March 4,1827.)

Smith, Sidney H. private July 2, 1861. Appointed 2d Cor poral August 15, 1862. Wounded at 2d Manassas,

Va. August 30, 1862. In hospital with diarrhoea May 1, 1864. Furloughed from General Hospital at Farmville, Va. for 40 days from July 22, 1864. No later record. (Born in Georgia October 1828.)

Speer, Joseph H. C. (Sug)- private July 2, 1861. Wounded at Seven Pines, Va. May 30, 1862. Transferred to C. S. Navy May 2,1864. Died of yellow fever at Charleston, S. C. October 1864.

Steighan, Frederick- private July 2, 1861. Captured at Fred- ericksburg, Va. December 13, 1862. Paroled at camp near Falmouth, Va. December 14,1862. No later record. (Born in Germany in 1822.)

Stewart, John M- private July 2, 1861. Admitted to General Hospital #9, at Richmond, Va. October 1862, and transferred to Chimborazo Hospital #4, there October 6, 1862. Furloughed to November 14,1862. No later record.

Sykes, Jacob- private July 2,1861. Discharged, over-age, at Camp Johnson, Va. January 7,1862.

Sykes, Thomas M. Y.- private July 2, 1861. Captured at Fred- ericksburg, Va. December 13, 1862. Paroled near Falmouth, Va. for exchange December 14,1862. Transferred to C. S. Navy May 2, 1864. In service at

Charleston, S. C., as oarsman, November 1864. No later record.

Taylor, John R.- private July 2,1861. Captured at Weldon Rail- road, Va. August 19,1864. Paroled at Elmira N. Y. March 14, 1865. Received at Boulware & Cox's Wharves, James River, Va. for exchange, March 18-21,1865. No later record.

Teel, Alvin- private July 2, 1861. Died August or September 10, 1862.

Thompson, James E.- private March 4, 1862. Wounded at Cedar Run, Va. August 9, 1862. Admitted to C. S. A. General Hospital at Charlottesville, Va. August 11, 1862, and died there of wounds September 16,1862.

Thompson, Joseph- private July 2,1861.

Thurman, John Michael- private July 2, 1861. Pension records show he was wounded in left side at Chancellorsville, Va. May 3, 1863; at Fort Harrison, Va. September 29,1864; Petersburg, Va. March 1865, and was at home on wounded furlough close of war.

Tidwell, M. M.- private July 2,1861. No later record.

Tomlinson, John I. (or John J.- private July 2, 1861. Ap- pointed Sergeant Major. "Paid for commutation of rations at dames Island, S. C., December 30,1863.

Tomlinson, Joseph P- private July 2,1861. Appointed Regimen- tal Musician. Captured near Columbus, Ga. April 18, 1865, and transferred to Military Prison at Macon, Ga., April 23, 1865. No later record.

Tomlinson, William- private July 2,1861.

Townsend, John L- private July 2,1861. Discharged, disability.

Underwood, Melbourn B.- private. Received pay at Atlanta, Ga. December 10,1862. No later record.

Underwood, William M.- private July 2, 1861. Wounded and captured at Fredericksburg, Va. December 13,1862. Exchanged. Sur rendered, Greensboro, N. C. April 26,1865.

Upchurch, Alfred V.- private July 2,1861. Killed at Mechanics- ville, Va. June 26,1862.

Varner, William D.- private July 2, 1861. Surrendered, Greens- boro, N. C. April 26,1865.

Walker, Americus V. (or Americus E.)- private July 2, 1861. Admitted to Danville, Va. hospital May 28, 1862.

Returned to duty June 18, 1862. Furloughed from Danville, Va. hospital for 60 days from November 7,1862. No later record.

Walker, Andrew W.- private July 2,1861. No later record.

Walker, George Washington- private July 2,1861. Surrendered, Greensboro, N. C. April 26,1865.

Walker, Silas L- private July 2,1861. No later record.

Ward, Edward M. T.- private July 2, 1861. Wounded at Mechanicsville, Va. June 26,1862. Died from wounds in 1862.

Whitaker, William H.- private July 2, 1861. Wounded at 2d Manassas, Va. August 30 1862. Surrendered, Greensboro, N. C. 26,1865.

Wilder, Larkin- private July 2, 1861. Captured at Sharpsburg, Md. September 17, 1862. Paroled at Fort McHenry, Md. and sent to Fortress Monroe, Va. for exchange November 1862. Exchanged at Aiken's Landing, Va. November 10,1862. No later record.

Wilkinson, - private 1862. Substitute for Peter Moseley. Wounded at Sharpsburg, Md. September 17, 1862. Died of wounds in 1862.

Williams, John R.- private July 2,1861. Captured at Fredericks- burg, Va. December 13,1862. Paroled for exchange December 17,1862. Surrendered, Greensboro, N. C. April 26,1865.

Wise, J. D. R.- private July 2,1861. No later record.

Wyatt, S. J.- private 1863. Discharged, Goldsboro, N. C.

The Georgia 22nd Infantry Regiment

This regiment was formed from Schley, Glascock, Bartow, Lincoln, Washington, Dawson, and Henry counties. It served in Wright's and Sorrel's Brigade.

The regiment lost 10 killed and 77 wounded at Oak Grove, 6 killed, 32 wounded, and 18 missing at Malvern Hill, 13 killed and 50 wounded as Second Manassas. There were 400 engaged at Gettysburg, and more than 40% were disabled. It sustained 25 casualties in route from Pennsylvania and 50 at Manassas Gap. It surrendered at Appomattox on 9 APR 1865 with 9 officers and 197 men.

Company K

Henry Volunteers

Albert, Joseph T. - Captain August 31,1861. Killed at 2d Manassas, Va. August 28,1862.

Callaway, Isaac W. - 1st Lieutenant August 31, 1861. Elected Captain August 30,1862. Wounded at Gettysburg, Pa. July 2,1863, and died result of amputation of leg in hospital there, July 18, 1863.

Owen, Westley C. (or Owens) - 2d Lieutenant August 31,1861. Died of typhoid fever in Chimborazo Hospital #3, at Richmond, Va. June 22,1862.

Alexander, Joseph W. - Enlisted as a private in Co.-, 2d Battn. Ga. Cavalry June 10, 1862. Transferred to Co. B, 5th Regiment Ga. Cavalry January 20,1863. Elected 2d Lieutenant of Co. K, 22d Regiment Ga. Inf. February 21,1863; 1st Lieutenant July 18,1863. Captured at Wilderness, Va. May 10,1864. Released at Fort Delaware, Del. May 10,1865.

George, David - Jr.2d Lieutenant August 31,1861. Resigned January 3,1862.

Clayton, Francis M. - 1st Sergeant August 31,1861. Elected Jr. 2d Lieutenant February 14, 1862; 1st

Lieutenant August 30, 1862; Captain July 18,1863. Surrendered, Appomattox, Va. April 9, 1865. (Born in Georgia in 1833.)

Dodson, George W.-2d Sergeant August 31 1861. Discharged, disability, at Camp Blanchard, Va. April 1,1862. Died at home June 1862.

Nolley, Timen M.-3d Sergeant August 31,1861.Died in Navy Hospital at Portsmouth, Va. December 18,1861.

Bowen, John N.-4th Sergeant August 31,1861. Wounded at 2d Manassas, Va. August 30,1862. Died of wounds in Staunton, Va. hospital September 21,1862. Buried there in Thornrose Cemetery.

Wallace, Simeon S.- Sergeant August 31,1861.Elected 1st Lieutenant October 4,1862; Captain July 30,1864. Paroled at Richmond, Va. April 18,1865.

Green, Henry F.-1st Corporal August 31, 1861. Appointed 4th Sergeant December 1862; 3d Sergeant in 1863. Wounded in leg at Gettysburg, Pa. July 2, 1863, and captured there July 5, 1863. Paroled at DeCamp General Hospital, David's Island, N. Y. Harbor, in 1863. Received at City Point, Va. for exchange September 16, 1863. Roll for February 28, 1865, last on file, shows him absent without leave since September 5th. Pension records show right leg was disabled at Petersburg, Va. July 30, 1864. (Born in Georgia October 9,1839. Died at McDonough, Ga. February 5,1926.)

Stephens, William Rufus-2d Corporal August 31, 1861. Missing at Gettysburg, Pa. July 2, 1863. Roll dated February 28, 1865, last on file, shows him absent; prisoner of war. No later record.

Albert, John J.-3d Corporal August 31, 1861. Appointed 2d Corporal in 1863. On furlough December 1864. Roll for February 28, 1865, last on file, shows him absent without leave since February 5, 1865. Pension records show he contracted diarrhoea in service and was at home on furlough close of war. (Born in Henry County, Ga. October 7,1845.)

Townsend, Littleton Dennis - 4th Corporal August 31, 1861. Captured at Gettysburg, Pa. July 2, 1863. Roll for February 28, 1865, last on file, shows him absent, prisoner of war. No later record.

Deal, Marcellus R.- Musician August 31, 1861. private in 1861. Discharged, disability, at Camp Blanchard, Va. December 5,1861.

Albert, Thomas M.- private August 31, 1861. Appointed 5th Sergeant December 1,1861. Killed at Gettysburg, Pa. July 2,1863.

Askew, Philetus N.- private March 26, 1862. Admitted to Chimborazo Hospital #4, at Richmond, Va., with typhoid fever, June 20,1862, and died there June 28,1862.

Askew, William H.- private March 3, 1862. Furloughed from hospital for 30 days November 6,1863. Unable to return to command.

Bartlett, George M.- private August 31, 1861. Discharged, disability, at Richmond, Va. January 31,1862.

Bentley, Oliver H.- private March 3,1862. Arm disabled at Gettysburg, Pa. July 2, 1863. Roll dated February 28, 1865, shows him "Absent, in Lee's Battn., wounded and lost use of arm."

Bentley, W. H. H. - private August 31, 1861. Appointed Sergeant. Died in Richmond, Va. hospital June 30,1862.

Bowden, John M.- private August 31, 1861. Appointed 1st Corporal in 1863. Wounded severely in mouth at North Anna River, Va. May 27, 1864.

Pension records show he was on detail duty as Enrolling Officer close of war. (Resident of Georgia since November 7,1842.)

Bowen, David C.- private August 31,1861. Killed at Malvern Hill, Va. July 1,1862.

Bowen, Elzy T.- private March 3, 1862. Killed at 2d Manassas, Va. August 30,1862.

Bowen, Marquis D.- private March 3, 1862. Wounded at Crater near Petersburg, Va. July 30, 1864. Captured at Deep Bottom, Va. August 16,1864. Died at Point Lookout, Md. September 9,1864.

Bowen, Noah James- private March 3, 1862. Roll for February 28, 1865, last on file, shows him absent on furlough for 24 days from February 17,1865. No later record. (Born in Georgia in 1835.)

Bowen, William H.- private August 31,1861. Wounded at Gettysburg, Pa. July 2, 1863. Surrendered, Appomattox, Va. April 9, 1865.

Brown, Loren S.- private May 8, 1862. Roll for February 28, 1865, last on file, shows him absent, detailed in hospital at Liberty, Va. No later record.

Callaway, John A.- private May 2,1862. Discharged, furnished Patrick Fitzgerald as substitute, February

20, 1863. Enlisted as a private in Co. D, 1st Regiment Ga. Inf. (Olmstead's), March 3, 1864. Captured at Marietta, Ga. June 19, 1864. Paroled at Camp Mor ton, Ind. and forwarded to Point Lookout, Md. for exchange March 10, 1865. Received at Boulware & Cox's Wharves, James River, Va., March 25,1865. No later record.

Carroll, Columbus C.- private August 31, 1861. Absent without leave September 1, 1864 - February 28, 1865. Pension records show he was sent to Atlanta, Ga. hospital with typhoid fever, date not given. Assigned to light duty with Lee's Battalion, and surrendered at Macon, Ga. in 1865. (Born in Georgia in 1840.)

Carroll, John H.- private March 3, 1862. Sent to General Hospital at Richmond, Va. in 1862. Died at Falling Creek, Va. in 1862.

Carroll, Josiah D.- private August 31, 1861. Deserted February 20, 1865. Received by Provost Marshal General, Washington, D. C., a Confederate deserter; took oath of allegiance to U. S. Govern ment and furnished transportation to Salem, Ill. February 27,1865.

Carroll, Needham J.- private August 31, 1861. Roll for February 28, 1865, last on file, shows him absent without leave since February 1 1865. Pension records show he left command on 30 days' sick furlough, at Petersburg, Va., March 1865. (Born in Georgia.)

Carroll, Richmond T.- private March 3, 1862. Wounded in arm, necessitating amputation, at Gettysburg, Pa. July 2, 1863. Captured in Henry County, Ga. November 16, 1864. Released at Point Lookout, Md. June 24,1865. (Born in Georgia February 14,1831.)

Carroll, William A.- private August 31, 1861. Wounded in 1862. Sent to General Hospital at Richmond, Va. in 1862. Received commutation of rations while on wounded furlough at his home in Georgia August 1-September 1, 1862. Killed at Gettysburg, Pa. July 2,1863.

Clarke, Amos J.- private August 31, 1861. Wounded at Deep Bottom, Va. August 16, 1864. Surrendered, Appomattox, Va. April 9,1865.

Clarke, David- private August 31, 1861. Sent to General Hospital at Richmond, Va. in 1862. Died at Winchester, Va. September 1862.

Clarke, Henry W.- private August 31,1861. Sent to General Hospi- tal at Richmond, Va. in 1862, and died there June 1862.

Clarke, Thomas A.- private August 31, 1861. Died of typhoid fever in General Hospital #18, Richmond, Va., June 29,1862.

Clarke, Warren J.- private May 7, 1862. Captured and paroled at Warrenton, Va. September 29,1862. Discharged, furnished William M. Riley as substitute, December 29,1862.

Clay, Henry J.- private August 31, 1861. Died of typhoid fever in Richmond, Va. hospital July 26,1862.

Coe, James N.- private May 2, 1862. Appointed Assistant Sur- geon at Brigade Hospital in 1862. Discharged on account of phthisis at Farmville, Va. November 20, 1862. Died at home June 1863.

Cook, John B.- private August 31, 1861. Wounded and captured at Gettysburg, Pa. July 2,1863. Exchanged. Captured at Amelia Court House, Va. April 5, 1865. Released at Point Lookout, Md. June 24,1865.

Crane, Samuel S.- private August 31,1861. Died in Richmond, Va. hospital June 27,1862.

Dodson, Felix F.- private August 31,1861. Reported "discharged" December 30, 1861, but "present" on roll dated February 28, 1862. Other records shows him "paid in full to May 1, 1862." Killed at Crater near Petersburg, Va. July 30,1864.

Doyal, William T.- private March 3, 1862. Deserted to enemy February 21, 1865. Received by Provost Marshal General, army of Potomac, a Confederate deserter, February 26, 1865. Took oath of allegiance to U. S. Govt. at Washington, D. C. March l,1865.

Duncan, Henry M.- private August 31, 1861. Discharged on ac- count of ill health, at Camp Blanchard, Va., December 30,1861.

Fitzgerald, Patrick- private February 20, 1863. Substitute for J.A. Calloway. Deserted at Fredericksburg, Va. June 14, 1863. Took oath of allegiance to U. S. Govt. at Washington, D. C. July 17,1863.

Ford, Napoleon E.- private August 31, 1861. Died of diarrhoea in General Hospital at Danville, Va. August 9,1862.

Gardner, William A.- private August 31, 1861. Wounded and captured at Gettysburg, Pa. July 3,1863. Transferred to U. S. A. General Hospital at Chester, Pa. for exchange August 17, 1863. Received at City Point, Va. August 20,1863. Roll for February

28,1865, last on file, shows him absent without leave since February 14, 1864. No later record.

George A. H.- private February 26. Captured and paroled at Gettys- burg, Pa. July 3, 1863. Surrendered, Appomattox, Va. April 9, 1865.

George, Levi J.- private August 31, 1861. Deserted, went home, July 23,1863.

George, Russell A.- private August 31,1861. Deserted, went home, March 12,1864.

Grant, Isaac M.- private August 31,1861. Sick in General Hospital at Richmond, Va. June 1862. Died at Falling Creek, Va. August 1862.

Grant, Reuben J.- private May 2,1862. Killed at Gettysburg, Pa. July 2,1863.

Grant, William M.- private August 31,1861. Captured and paroled at Williamsport, Md. July 6, 1863. Surrendered, Appomattox, Va. April 9,1865.

Green, Samuel Patterson- private May 5,1862. Roll for February 28, 1865, last on file, shows him absent without leave since August 1,1864. Pension records show he was detailed to wagon train. Permanently disabled by heavy lifting while wagon trains were miring on retreat from Pennsylvania, in 1863.

Contracted liver trouble and other physical disabilities in service, which rendered him unfit for further duty. (Born in Ga. July 4,1837.) ?

Green, William A.- private August 31,1861. Wounded at Sharps- burg, Md. September 17,1862. Admitted to Chimborazo Hospital #5, at Richmond, Va. October 1, 1862. Returned to duty November 26, 1862. Killed at Gettysburg, Pa. July 2,1863.

Hardin, James L- private February 26,1862. Wounded and disabled at Sharpsburg, Md. September 17,1862. Surrendered, Appomattox, Va. April 9,1865.

Helms, John A.- private August 31,1861.Killed at Seven Pines, Va. June 30,1862.

Henry, E. Z.- private August 31,1861. Killed at Gettysburg, Pa. July 2,1863.

Hinton,William J.(or W. T.)- private February 28,1862. Died at Richmond, Va. in 1862.

Hooks, Martin V.- private August 31,1861. Wounded in hip at Sharpsburg, Md. September 17,1862. Surrendered, Appomattox, Va. April 9,1865. (Born in DeKalb County, Ga. October 1,1840.)

Howell, James- private August 31,1861. Surrendered, Appomat- tox, Va. April 9,1865.

Johnson, James C.- private December 9,1862. Sent to hospital August 1864. Died of chronic diarrhoea in C. S.A. General Hospital at Danville, Va. October 11,1864.

Johnson, John C.- private August 31,1861. Discharged prior to April 1862. Died at home in 1862.

Kelly, Thomas- private August 31,1861. Died of typhoid fever in Chimborazo Hospital #3, at Richmond, Va. June 27,1862.

Kitchens, Thomas J.- private March 31,1864. Paroled at Farmville, Va. April 11-21,1865.

Livingston, Loren B.- private August 31,1861. Wounded at Chan- cellorsville, Va. May 3,1863; Cold Harbor, Va. June 3,1864. Sur rendered, Appomattox, Va. April 9,1865.

Livingston, L. M.- private August 31, 1861. Wounded at Cold Harbor, Va. June 3,1864. Roll for February 28,1865, last on file, shows him absent without leave since October 1st. No later record.

Lowe, James P.- private August 31, 1861. Discharged at Falling Creek, Va. July 27,1862.

Masters, Griffin S.- private August 31, 1861. Killed at Crater near Petersburg, Va. July 30,1864.

McCulley, James C.- private December 9, 1862. Died of fever in General Hospital #3, at Lynchburg, Va. August 17, 1863. Buried there in Confederate Cemetery. No. 8, 1st Line, Lot 196 Ferguson's.

McGarity, Jeremiah A.- private February 26, 1862. Wounded at 2d Manassas, Va. August 28, 1862. Surrendered, Appomattox, Va. April 9,1865. (Born in Georgia April 15,1835.)

McGarity, John M.- private September 17, 1861. Wounded at Cold Harbor, Va. June 23, 1864. Roll dated February 28, 1865, last on file, shows him "Absent, sent to hospital wounded, November 1864." No later record. (Born in Georgia in 1838.)

McGarity, Thomas F.- private February 26 1862. Roll dated February 28, 1865, last on file, shows him absent, sent to hospital March 1864. Pension records show he was discharged, disability, September 1864.

McKee, Madison Church- private May 7, 1862. Surrendered, Appomattox, Va. April 9,1865.

McKee, Samuel Payne- private August 31, 1861. Died of typhoid fever in Chimborazo Hospital #1, at Richmond, Va. July 1, 1862.

Mosley, Henry S.- private September 16, 1861. Appointed 5th Ser- geant July 2, 1863. Wounded at Gettysburg, Pa. July 2, 1863. Appears last on roll for December 1863.

Nix, J. Allman- private May 7, 1862. Died of typhoid fever in Chimborazo Hospital #2, at Richmond, Va. June 14,1862.

Nix, John J.- private September 16, 1861. Died while home on furlough subsequent to April 30,1862.

Norris, John E.- private August 31, 1861. Surrendered, Appomat- tox, Va. April 9,1865.

Owen, Emory M. (or Owens)- private August 31,1861. Appointed 3d Corporal in 1863. Surrendered, Appomattox, Va. April 9,1865.

Owen, J. S. (or Owens)- private August 31, 1861. Surrendered, Appomattox, Va. April 9,1865.

Owen, Newsom T. (or Owens)- private April 3, 1862. Died in General Hospital at Richmond, Va. June 29,1862.

The Pattillo Brothers from Henry County, Georgia, ¼ plate ambrotype, by unknown photographer. The four brothers, each holding a D- guard Bowie or side knife, (left to right) Benjamin, George, James and John were all members of the 22nd Georgia.

http://www.southernmuseum.org/exhibits_travelin gexhibits.htm

Pattillo, Benjamin H.- private July 26, 1862. Killed at 2d Manassas, Va. August 30,1862.

Pattillo, George M. T.- private September 16, 1861. On detail duty in shoe shops at Augusta, Ga. from 1863, to close of war.

Pattillo, James M. - private September 16, 1861. Discharged March 1862. Reenlisted. Wounded in foot, resulting in amputation of third toe, at Deep Bottom, Va. August 16, 1864. Pension records show he was at home on wounded furlough close of war. (Born in Henry County, Ga. May 3,1835.)

Pattillo, John R. J.- private August 31, 1861. Wounded at Seven Days' Fight near Richmond, Va. in 1862. Admitted to Chim borazo Hospital #2, Richmond, Va. May 31, 1862. Returned to duty June 14, 1862. Admitted to C. S. A. General Hospital at Charlottesville, Va. November 20, 1862. Admitted to same hospital December 16,1862. Returned to duty December 17, 1862. Pension records show he was discharged on account of wounds March 1863.

Phillips, Harris Jesse- private August 31,1861. Wounded at Petersburg, Va. June 23, 1864. Furloughed for 60 days August 3, 1864. Roll for February 28, 1865, last on file, shows him absent without leave September 1, 1864. No later record. (Born in Georgia December 23, 1837.)

Phillips, William A.- private May 7, 1862. Wounded and captured at Gettysburg, Pa. July 3,1863. Paroled at Point Lookout, Md. February 18,1865. No later record.

Pope, Joel Crawford- private March 1862. Discharged, disability, at Portsmouth, Va. in 1863. (Born in Georgia August 19,1834.)

Pope, W. F.- private March 1862. Admitted to Jackson Hospital at Richmond, Va. May 28, 1864, and died there of acute diarrhoea July 12,1864. Buried there in Hollywood Cemetery.

Pritchett, John W.- private August 31,1861. Died at Portsmouth, Va. January 7,1862.

Ragan, James H.- private July 25, 1862. Killed at Gettysburg, Pa. July 2,1863.

Ray, Thomas N.- private September 16, 1861. Wounded at Gettysburg, Pa. July 2, 1863, and died of wounds in hospital there July 10,1863.

Ray, W. W.- private March 3, 1862. Surrendered Appomattox, Va. April 9,1865.

Richards, John R. (or John A.)-Enlisted as a private in Co. G, 19th Regiment Ga. Inf. July 2, 1861. Appointed Color Corporal July 1861. Transferred to Co. K, 22d Regiment Ga. Inf. March 1,1862. Discharged on account of dropsy at Falling Creek, Va. July 17, 1862.

Riley, William M.- private December 29,1862. Substitute for Warren J. Clarke. Captured at

Gettysburg, Pa. July 2, 1863. Roll for February 28, 1865, last on file, shows him absent, a prisoner of war. No later record.

Robertson, Bennett B.- private May 7, 1862. Died in General Hospital at Richmond, Va. August 13,1862.

Robertson, Noel R. (or Novell R.)- private August 31, 1861. Died of disease in Richmond, Va. November 3,1862.

Sappington, David M.- private August 31, 1861. Died in Portsmouth, Va. hospital December 30,1861.

Simpkins, James H.- private August 31, 1861. Died at Richmond, Va. July 1,1862.

Simpkins, Robert B.- private August 31,1861. Admitted to C.S.A. General Hospital at Charlottesville, Va., on account of debility, December 16,1862. Returned to duty March 4,1863. Killed at Gettysburg, Pa. July 2,1862.

Simpson, James A.- private August 31,1861. Appointed 4th Corporal in 1861. Elected 2d Lieutenant June 22,1862. Resigned, disability, February 21,1863. Pension records show he enlisted as a private in Co. B,2d Regiment Ga. Reserve Inf. July

1864. Name not found on this regiment. Surrendered, Atlanta, Ga. April 9, 1865. (Born in Georgia.)

Sims, James N.- private August 31,1861. Discharged, disability, May 24,1862.

Skelton, Charles S.- private August 31,1861. Captured at Deep Bottom, Va. August 17,1864. Paroled at Point Lookout, Md. and transferred to Aiken's Landing, Va. for exchange March 14,1865. Received at Boulware s Wharf, James River, Va., March 16,1865. No later record.

Skinner, H. J.- private August 31,1861. Surrendered, Appomattox, Va. April 9,1865.

Smith, John C.- private October 30,1861. Wounded in Seven Days' Fight, near Richmond, Va. June 26,1862. Died of wounds in General Hospital #21, at Richmond, Va. June 26,1862.

Sorrow, F. L.- private March 3, 1862. Died in Richmond, Va. hospital July 8,1862.

Sprayberry, Ferdinand G.- private August 31, 1861. Admitted to General Hospital #18, at Richmond, Va. with typhoid fever, June 28,1862. Returned to duty July 22,1862. Killed at Gettys burg, Pa. July 2,1863.

Sprayberry, Robert E.- private August 31,1861. Discharged December 27,1861.

Sprayberry, Uphrates A. V.- private August 31,1861. Wounded and captured at Gettysburg, Pa. July 2,1863. Took oath of alle giance to U. S. Govt. and enlisted in U. S. service, under name of W. A. B. Sprayberry, February 26,1864.

Stanley, A. J.- private August 31,1861. Surrendered, Appomattox, Va. April 9,1865.

Stanley, Bithum L- private September 1863. Surrendered, Appomattox, Va. April 9,1865. (Born in Georgia. Died in Fulton County, Ga. April 27,1930.)

Stanley, Eli- private May 7,1862. Wounded and disabled at 2d Manassas, Va. August 30,1862.Received pay at Petersburg, Va. February 16,1865. No later record. (Born in Georgia October 28, 1832.)

Stanley, Jesse- private February 26,1862. Killed at Petersburg, Va. June 25,1864.

Stanley, John J.- private February 26,1862. Wounded at 2d Ma- nassas, Va. August 30,1862. Roll for February 28,1865, last on file, shows him present. No later record.

Stanley, John M.- private April 28,1862. Wounded and permanently disabled, date and place unknown. Appears last on roll for December 1863.

Stanley, J. B.- private August 31, 1861. Captured at Gettysburg, Pa. July 2, 1863. Died of typhoid fever at Fort Delaware, Del. August 13,1863.

Stanley, J. G.- private August 31, 1861. Sick in General Hospital at Richmond, Va. June 1862. Killed at Gettysburg, Pa. July 2, 1863.

Stanley, Laudrick (or Loderick)- private July 1,1864. Wounded in right breast at Crater near Petersburg, Va. July 30, 1864. (Born in Georgia February 25,1845.)

Stanley, Levi- private February 28, 1862. Wounded at Seven Days' Fight near Richmond, Va. June 25, 1862. Absent, wounded, June 30,1862. No later record.

Stanley, William B.- private May 2, 1862. Wounded at Fredericksburg, Va. December 13, 1862. Captured at Gettysburg, Pa. July 2,1863. Died at Fort Delaware, Del. August 14,1863.

Stephenson, William M.- private August 31, 1861. Appointed 1st Sergeant. Discharged at Falling Creek, Va. July 13,1862.

Stewart, J. M.- private July 2, 1862. Wounded, captured and paroled, at Gettysburg, Pa. July 2,1863. Roll for February 26, 1865, last on file, shows him absent without leave February 1st. No later record.

Sykes, W. L.- private July 2, 1862. Wounded in right arm, necessitating amputation, at Chancellorsville, Va. May 3, 1863. Discharged, disability, December 31,1863.

Tanner, Josiah G.- private August 31, 1861. Killed at Petersburg, Va. in 1864.

Thompson, Lemuel Harris- private August 31, 1861. Appointed 1st Sergeant in 1863. Wounded in arm necessitating amputa tion, and captured at Gettysburg, Pa. July 2, 1863. Paroled at Baltimore, Md. August 23, 1863. Received at City Point, Va. for exchange August 24, 1863. (Born June 1, 1838. Died about May 27,1912.)

Thompson, Samuel M.- private February 26, 1862. Died of typhoid fever in Chimborazo Hospital #4, at Richmond, Va. July 4, 1862.

Tidwell, Mathew M.- private August 31, 1861. Killed in skirmish near Petersburg, Va. February 7,1865.

Townsend, John L.- private March 3,1862. Received pay at Camp near Fredericksburg, Va. for commutation of rations while on furlough from March 3, to April 15, 1862, on March 26, 1863. No later record.

Townsend, Odum L- private August 31, 1861. Discharged, disability, January 19,1863.

Walden, Robert, Jr. (or Waldin)- private August 31,1861. Wounded. Surrendered, Appomattox, Va. April 9,1865.

Waldrup, J. C.- private August 31, 1861. Captured, date and place unknown. Roll for February 28, 1865, last on file, shows him absent, prisoner of war. No later record.

White, John W.- private August 31, 1861. Appointed 2d Sergeant in 1863. Wounded at Petersburg, Va. in 1864. Surrendered, Ap pomattox, Va. April 9,1865. (Born in Georgia February 22,1840.)

White, Thomas A.- private May 7,1862. Killed or captured at Gettysburg, Va. July 2,1863.

Whitley, Francis N.- private August 31,1861. Killed at Chancellorsville, Va. May 3,1863.

Whitley, Marion W.- private August 31,1861. Died in Richmond, Va. hospital December 17,1861.

Wilkinson, Joseph N.- private August 31,1861. Appointed 4th Sergeant in 1863. Wounded and captured at Gettysburg, Pa. July 2,1863. Paroled at DeCamp General Hospital, David's Island, N. Y. Harbor, August 24,1863. Received at City Point, Va. for exchange August 28,1863. Wounded at Crater near Petersburg, Va. July 30,1864. Pension records show he was at home on wounded furlough close of war. (Born in Georgia April 17,1840.)

Wilkinson, Robert M.- private October 5,1861. Surrendered, Appomattox, Va. April 9,1865. (Born in Henry County, Ga. September 4,1837.)

Wilson, Augustus J.- private September 19,1861. Sick in General Hospital at Richmond, Va. June 1862. No later record. (Born in Henry County, Ga. Died in Atlanta, Ga. June 11,1899.)

Wilson, David- private March 4,1862. Surrendered, Appomattox, Va. April 9,1865.(Born in Georgia August 15,1834.)

The Georgia 44ᵗʰ Infantry Regiment

The Georgia 44th Infantry Regiment completed its organization at Camp Stephens, near Griffin, Georgia, in March, 1862. It was formed from Henry, Jasper, Clarke, Clayton, Spalding, Putnam, Fayette, Pike, Morgan, and Greene counties.   Two companies – A and I were formed from Henry County

The 44th was first sent on April 4ᵗʰ to Goldsboro, North Carolina on April 4ᵗʰ. It was combined with the 3rd Arkansas, the 1st North Carolina and the 3rd North Carolina to form a brigade under Brig. Gen. John G. Walker, in the division of Maj. Gen. Theophilus H. Holmes.

After the Seven Days Battles, Brig. Gen. Roswell Ripley succeeded Walker at the helm, and Maj. Gen. D. H. Hill assumed command of the division. The 44ᵗʰ served in General Ripley's, Doles', and Cook's Brigade, and fought with the Army of Northern Virginia from the Seven Days' Battles through the remainder of the war in Virginia.

Company A

This company suffered severely in the war. Only 5 men were present at Appomattox:

Private D. B. Dees,
J. W. Derrick,
J. C. Doolen,
M. Hubbard,
M. T. Turner.

Peebles, William H.- Captain March 4, 1862. Appointed Surgeon July 1862. Elected Major March 4, 1863; Lieutenant Colonel May 26, 1863; Colonel September 11, 1863. Captured at Spotsylvania, Va. May 10, 1864. Exchanged at Charleston Harbor, S. C. August 3, 1864. Wounded at Winchester, Va. September 19, 1864; furloughed. On way to rejoin command when war closed. (Died at Hampton, Ga. October 1, 1885.)

McKenzie, Augustus D.- 1st Lieutenant March 4, 1862. Elected Captain March 4, 1863. Captured at Gettysburg, Pa. July 4, 1863. Sent to Johnson's Island, O. July 18, 1863, and paroled there February 1865. Forwarded to Point Lookout, Md. for ex change March 14, 1865. Received at Boulware & Cox's

Wharves, James River, Va., March 22, 1865. (Born in Harris County, Ga. February 21, 1831.)

Credille, Henry M.- 2d Lieutenant March 4, 1862. Elected Captain July 1862. Wounded at Sharpsburg, Md. September 17, 1862. Wounded in arm, necessitating amputation, at Chancellorsville, Va. May 2, 1863. Died of wounds May 4, 1863. 728

Wilkins, Samuel J.- Jr. 2d Lieutenant March 4, 1862. Elected 2d Lieutenant July 1862. Wounded at Chancellorsville, Va. May 2, 1863; Gettysburg, Pa. July 4, 1863. Died. of wounds July 7, 1863.

Moore, Charles W.- 1st Sergeant March 4, 1862. Wounded at Ellison's Mill, Va. June 26, 1862. Died, while home on furlough, in Clayton County, Ga. July 28, 1862.

Adams, Thomas J.- 2d Sergeant March 4, 1862. Captured at Harper's Ferry, W. Va. July 8, 1864. Paroled at Elmira, N. Y. and transferred for exchange October 11, 1864. Received at Venus Point, Savannah River, Ga., November 15, 1864. Captured and paroled at Hartwell, Ga. May 17, 1865.

Strickland, Leroy - 3d Sergeant March 4, 1862. Killed near Washington, D. C. July 12, 1864.

Adams, William J. (Boss) - 4th Sergeant March 4, 1862. Appointed Quartermaster Sergeant. Wounded in knee in Virginia in 1864. Died of wounds in Jackson Hospital at Richmond, Va. June 4, 1864. Buried there in Hollywood Cemetery.

Derrick, James Wyatt - 5th Sergeant March 4, 1862. Wounded in left shoulder and permanently disabled at Sharpsburg, Md. September 17, 1862. Surrendered at Appomattox, Va. April 9, 1865. (Born September 18, 1830.)

Derrick, William D.- 1st Corporal March 4, 1862. Wounded at Ellison's Mill, Va. June 26, 1862; Fredericksburg, Va. December 13, 1862. Discharged on account of wound in right leg, at camp near Fredericksburg, Va., December 28, 1862. (Born October 12, 1837.)

Peebles, Henry H.- 2d Corporal March 4, 1862. Wounded at Chancellorsville, Va. May 2, 1863. Right leg permanently disabled at Spotsylvania, Va. May 10, 1864. Roll dated August 31, 1864, last on file, shows him absent, wounded. (Born in Ga. June 18, 1838.)

Moore, Jesse G.- 3d Corporal March 4, 1862. Died of fever in Chimborazo Hospital #5, at Richmond, Va. July 19, year not given.

Ponder, George M.- 4th Corporal March 4 1862. Appointed 1st Corporal December 28, 1862; 5th Sergeant in 1864. Captured at Spotsylvania, Va. May 10, 1864. Paroled at Fort Delaware, Del. February 1865. Exchanged March 7, 1865. Received at Boulware & Cox's Wharves, James River, Va., March 10-12, 1865. Died in Henry County, Ga.

Adams, John W.- private March 4, 1862. Elected Jr. 2d Lieutenant July 15, 1862. In General Hospital #1, at Lynchburg, Va. August 22, 1862. Elected 1st Lieutenant March 4, 1863. Furloughed for 24 days March 28, 1864. Wounded in 1864. Died of wounds at Kingsville, W. Va. or Richmond, Va., July 29, 1864.

Akins, Crockery Elijah - private March 4, 1862. Killed at Elli- son's Mill, Va. June 26, 1862.

Amis, W. W.- private March 4, 1862.

Anderson, Rowan C. (or Roan) - private March 4, 1862. Died of measles at Goldsboro, N. C. May 25, 1862.

Babb, John C.- private March 4, 1862. Died of fever in General Hospital at Camp Winder, Richmond, Va., September 20, 1862. Buried there in Hollywood Cemetery.

Bankston, John - private March 4, 1862.

Bankston, William - private March 17, 1862. Died of chronic diarrhea in General Hospital #2, at Lynchburg, Va. March 10, 1863. Buried there in Confederate Cemetery. Disinterred and sent to Jonesboro, Ga.

Bernard, William P.- private March 4, 1862. Wounded and captured at Silver Springs, Md. July 13, 1864. Died of wounds in Lincoln General Hospital at Washington, D. C. July 22, 1864. Buried at Arlington, Va.

Bridges, J. C.- private May 8, 1862. Wounded in left hip at Ellison's Mill, Va. June 26, 1862. Discharged, disability, at camp near Fredericksburg, Va., January 26, 1863. (Born in Henry County, Ga. February 28, 1835.)

Bunn, G. W.- private in 1862. Wounded at Ellison's Mill, Va. June 26, 1862.

Bunn, Joseph L.- private March 4, 1862. Captured at Fair- field, Pa. July 5, 1863. Took oath of allegiance to U. S. Govt. and released January 29, 1864.

Cagle, David - private May 5, 1862. Furloughed for 25 days from Winder Hospital, Division 3, at Richmond,

Va., November 15, 1862. Died of disease while home on furlough January 1, 1863.

Cagle, William W.- private August 6, 1862. Wounded at Chancellorsville, Va. May 2, 1863. Died of wounds May 4, 1863.

Callaway, James Sandford - private March 4, 1862. Wounded at Chancellorsville Va. May 2, 1863. Wounded in 1864. Died of wounds in Jackson Hospital at Richmond, Va. June 1, 1864. Buried there in Hollywood Cemetery.

Callaway, Jonathan Burton - private March 4, 1862. Discharged, on account of rheumatism, at Camp Walker near Richmond, Va., June 20, 1862. Died in Henry County, Ga.

Camp, Aaron N.- private August 6, 1862. Wounded in 1864. Roll dated August 31, 1864, last on file, shows him absent, wounded. No later record.

Carmichael, James C.- private May 5, 1862. Wounded at Chancellorsville, Va. May 2, 1863. Captured at Petersburg, Va. April 3, 1865. Released at Hart's Island, New York Harbor, June 15, 1865. (Born in Butts County, Ga. August 27, 1837.)

Carmichael, Samuel H.- private March 4, 1862. Severely wounded at Spotsylvania, Va. May 10, 1864. On wounded furlough August 1864. Captured near Petersburg, Va. March 25, 1865. Released at Point Lookout, Md. June 4, 1865.

Cloud, Cullen - private. Recruit. Died of disease at Winchester, Va. in 1863.

Cooper, Jarratt T. (or Jarrett T.) - private September 24, 1863. Wounded in 1864. Died of wounds, April 23, 1864.

Credille, Cullen G.- Enlisted as a private in Co. D, 2d Battn. Ga. Inf. August 8, 1861. Transferred to Co. A, 44th Regiment Ga. Inf. May 18, 1862. Captured at Spotsylvania, Va. May 5, 1864. Paroled at Fort Delaware, Del. February 1865. Received at Boulware & Cox's Wharves, James River, Va. March 10-12, 1865. Admitted to Jackson Hospital at Richmond, Va., with bronchitis March 13, 1865. Furloughed for 30 days March 28, 1865.

Credille, James M.- private May 8, 1862. Discharged, disability, at Camp Ripley, July 29, 1862. (Born in Henry County, Ga. in 1832.)

Credille, Josiah P.- private March 4, 1862. Killed at Malvern, Hill, Va. July 1, 1862.

Daniel, Cicero H.- private March 4, 1862. Wounded, right leg permanently disabled, at Sharpsburg, Md. September 17, 1862. Roll dated August 31, 1864, last on file, shows him present. (Born in Ga. June 7, 1833.)

Daniel, Henry A.- private March 4, 1862. Died July 28, 1862.

Darsey, George M. T.- private March 4, 1862. Died of pneumonia in Henningsen Hospital at Richmond, Va. February 15, 1863.

Darsey, John T.- private May 5, 1862. Captured at Peters- burg, Va. April 3, 1865. Released at Hart's Island, N. Y. Harbor, June 15, 1865. (Born in Ga. in 1839.)

Deas, Daniel B.- private March 4, 1862. Wounded at Boonesboro, Md. September 14, 1862. Surrendered at Appomattox, Va. April 9, 1865.

Deas, Henry T.- Enlisted as a private in Co. D, 3d Battn. Ga. State Troops February 11, 1862. Roll for April 17, 1862, last on file, shows him present. Mustered out April 1862. Enlisted as a private in Co. A, 44th Regiment Ga. Inf. in 1862. Appointed 4th Corporal tune 1864. Wounded June 1864. Roll dated August 31, 1864, last on file, shows him at home on wounded furlough. No later record.

Deas, Simeon Asberry - private March 4, 1862. Wounded in right hip at Spotsylvania, Va. May 10, 1864. Roll dated August 31, 1864, last on file, shows him absent, wounded. (Born in Ga. January 19, 1838.)

Derrick, John G.- private March 4, 1862. Appointed 2d Sergeant in 1862. Discharged, furnished substitute. Died in Fulton County, Ga. in 1891.

Derrick, Thomas S.- private April 30, 1862. Wounded at Chancellorsville, Va. May 2, 1863. Died of wounds in General Hospital #16, at Richmond, Va. June 16, 1863.

Derrick (Derick), Wallace J.- private July 11, 1862. Severely wounded in right thigh and arm at Sharpsburg, Md. September 17, 1862, and captured there September 28, 1862. Exchanged at City Point, Va. February 18, 1863. Discharged at Atlanta, Ga., on account of gunshot wound which caused shortening of right leg, July 31, 1863. (Resident of Ga. since April 23, 1844. Died April 9, 1917.)

Driver, Charles - private March 4, 1862. Discharged, disability, May 23, 1862.

Dulin, John C. (or Doolin) - private October 15, 1862. Captured at Winchester, Va. September 19, 1864. Sent to Point Lookout, Md. and paroled there February 10,

1865. Received at Cox's Landing, James River, Va. for exchange, February 14, 1865. Surrendered at Appomattox, Va. April 9, 1865.

Farmer, Charles - private. Recruit.

Farmer, William H.- private March 4, 1862. Discharged on account of hemorrhage of lungs, at Camp McIntosh near Goldsboro, N. C., May 24, 1862.

Fields, Amaziah H.- private March 4, 1862. Died of typhoid fever in Chimborazo Hospital #5, at Richmond, Va., August 18, 1862.

Gay, Jacob - private September 24, 1863. Wounded in scalp in 1864. Died of wounds and paralysis in Jackson Hospital at Richmond, Va. June 4, 1864. Buried there in Hollywood Cemetery.

Gibson, Harrison - private. Recruit.

Gibson, James - private. Recruit. Killed at Spotsylvania, Va. May 10, 1864.

Gibson, Patrick - private. Recruit. Killed at Spotsylvania, Va. May 10, 1864.

Gice, Joseph - See Guice.

Goss, Eaby. See Goss, Yerby A.

Goss, Thomas Monroe - private March 4, 1862. Wounded at Sharpsburg, Md. September 17, 1862. Captured at Spotsylvania, Va. May 10, 1864. Paroled at Fort Delaware, Del. February 1865. Received at Boulware & Cox's Wharves, James River, Va.,

March 10-12, 1865. (Born in Ga. March 1847. Died in Henry County, Ga. in 1917.)

Goss, Yerby A.- private May 8, 1862. Died of measles at Richmond, Va. August 7, 1862.

Grant, Benjamin F.- private March 4, 1862. Under age. Not mustered in.

Gray, Thomas J.- private March 4, 1862. Under age. Not mustered in.

Green, Crawford - private March 4, 1862. Captured June 1864. Paroled at Fort Delaware, Del. October 30, 1864. Received at Venus Point, Savannah River, Ga. for exchange, November 15, 1864.

Juice, Joseph - private March 4, 1862. Wounded, right arm permanently disabled, at Winchester, Va. September 19, 1864. Pension records show he was at home on wounded furlough close of war. (Born in Clayton County, Ga. March 27, 1844. Died in Confederate Soldiers' Home at Atlanta, Ga. April 5,

1927. Buried in Confederate Cemetery at Marietta, Ga.)

Hand, James Henderson - private May 8, 1862. Captured at Cedar Creek, Va. October 19, 1864. Sent to Point Lookout, Md. October 23, 1864. No later record.

Hardegree, Hiram - private May 8, 1862. Died of typhoid pneumonia, Ferguson's, January 11, 1863. Buried in Confederate Cemetery at Lynchburg, Va. No. 5, Line 5, Lot 79.

Harper, Roderick Henry - private March 4, 1862. Wounded at Ellison's Mill, Va. June 26, 1862. Contracted small pox and sent to hospital. (Born in Henry County, Ga. in 1830.)

Harris, James E.- private March 4, 1862. Wounded at Elli- son's Mill, Va. June 26, 1862. Died of wounds June 30, 1862.

Henry, Reuben H.- private March 4, 1862. Absent sick, July - August 1864. Retired December 20, 1864. Attached to hospital as nurse January 27, 1865. (Born in Henry County, Ga. in 1830. Died in Fulton County, Ga. in 1925.)

Hopkins, Hugh E.- private March 4, 1862. Died in Winchester, Va. hospital October 30, 1862.

Hubbard, Marshall C.- private March 4, 1862. Wounded in abdomen and left leg at Chancellorsville, Va. May 2, 1863. Surrendered at Appomattox, Va. April 9, 1865. (Born in Henry County, Ga. March 29, 1828.)

Jackson, Edmund E.- private March 4, 1862. Appointed 4th Corporal in 1862; 3d Corporal in 1864. Wounded in left thigh and captured at Spotsylvania, Va. May 10, 1864. Released at Fort Delaware, Del. June 16, 1865. (Born in Ga. June 1, 1837.)

Jackson, John R.- private March 4, 1862. Appointed 2d Corporal. Captured at Gettysburg, Pa. July 1 or 4, 1863. Paroled at DeCamp General Hospital at David's Island, N. Y. Harbor in 1863. Received at City Point, Va. September 8, 1863. Appointed 1st Corporal in 1864. Wounded in shoulder, resulting in paralysis of right arm, at Wilderness, Va. May 6, 1864. Roll for July -August 1864, last on file, shows him absent wounded. (Born in Ga. March 1, 1841.)

Jackson, Roderick W.- private March 4, 1862. Transferred to Co. I. Died of disease at Charlottesville, Va. December 12, 1863. Buried there in Confederate Cemetery.

Jackson, Sandford - private. Recruit.

Jarrett, J. H.- private May 18, 1864. Admitted to General Hospital #9, Richmond, Va. September 16, 1864. Pension records show he was at home on furlough close of war. (Born in Henry County, Ga. in 1841.)

Jarrett, William J. (or William T.) - private September 8, 1863. Captured at Spotsylvania, Va. May 10, 1864. Paroled at Fort Delaware, Del. February 1865, and released there June 16, 1865.

Jenkins, John H.- private March 4, 1862. Died June 28, 1862.

Johnson, Thomas D. F.- private March 4, 1862. Killed at Elli- son's Mill, Va. June 26, 1862.

Joiner, Seaborn Bennett W.- private September 24, 1863. Died of typhoid fever at Harrisonburg, Va. August 23, 1864. Buried in Virginia.

Jones, John M.- private August 13, 1862. Substitute for William Jones. Wounded in right leg, necessitating amputation, at Chancellorsville, Va. May 2, 1863. Roll for July -August 1864, last on file, shows him home on wounded furlough. At home wounded close of war.

(Resident of Ga. since August 31, 1947. Died at Stockbridge, Ga. June 25, 1915.)

Jones, William - private March 4, 1862. Discharged, furnished John M. Jones as substitute, August 13, 1862.

Kimbell, John K.- private August 6, 1862. Discharged, defective eyesight, January 3, 1863. Served as Enrolling Officer until close of war. (Born in Ga. in 1840.)

Linder, Thompson D. T.- private May 5, 1862. Appointed 4th Sergeant May 5, 1862. Captured at Spotsylvania, Va. May 10, 1864. Appointed 3d Sergeant in 1864. Died of small pox at Fort Delaware, Del. July 5, 1864.

Little, Adam E.- See Co. E.

Little, Demosthenes C.- private March 4, 1862. Captured at Spotsylvania, Va. May 10, 1864. Released at Fort Delaware, Del. June 16, 1865.

Little, Zabud M.- private March 4, 1862. Transferred to Co. E, in exchange for Adam E. Little, March 1862. Roll of Texas Hospital at Auburn, Ala., dated June 30, 1864, shows him present.

Lowery, George L.- private February 26, 1864. Captured at Petersburg, Va. March 25, 1865. Released at Point Lookout, Md. June 4, 1865.

Lowery, Jackson - Enlisted as a private in Co. D, 3d Battn. Ga. State Troops November 18, 1861. Roll for April 17, 1862, last on file, shows him present. Mustered out in 1862. Enlisted as a private in Co. A, 44th Regiment Ga. Inf. April 10, 1863. Appointed 2d Sergeant June 1864. Roll for July -August 1864, last on file, shows him present. No later record.

Mills, R. L.- private. Recruit.

Minter, Richard H.- private. Recruit. Wounded at Chancellorsville, Va. May 2, 1863; in right shoulder at Gettysburg, Pa. July 1, 1863, and captured there July 5, 1863. Paroled at DeCamp General Hospital, David's Island, New York Harbor, and exchanged at City Point, Va. September 16, 1863. Received pay at Richmond, Va. March 21, 1864. No later record. (Resident of Ga. since February 22, 1838.)

Moore, Henry M.- private May 8, 1862. Discharged, disability, July 18, 1862. Died in Clayton County, Ga. November 1900.

Moore, James - private. Killed in service.

Moore, Robert - private March 4, 1862. Discharged, under-age, October 24, 1862.

Moore, Robert A.- private March 4, 1862. Killed at Spotsylvania, Va. May 10, 1864.

Moore, Sanford R.- private March 4, 1862. Elected 2d Lieu- tenant May 4, 1863. Killed at Spotsylvania, Va. May 10, 1864.

Moore, Thomas S. (or Thomas L.) - private March 4, 1862. Killed near Richmond, Va. June 26, 1862.

Morris, William Jasper - private March 4, 1862. Wounded in right hip at Gettysburg, Pa. July 3, 1863. Captured at Spotsylvania, Va. May 10, 1864. Exchanged at Fort Delaware, Del. October 30, 1864. Received at Venus Point, Savannah River, Ga., November 15, 1864. No later record.

Nixon, William J.- private May 15, 1862. Appointed 5th Sergeant May 1862; 4th Sergeant in 1864. Captured at Spotsylvania, Va. May 10, 1864. Exchanged at Fort Delaware, Del. March 7, 1865. Received at Boulware & Cox's Wharves, James River, Va., March 10-12, 1865.

Orr, John S.- private March 4, 1862. Captured at Spotsylvania, Va. May 10, 1864. Paroled at Fort

Delaware, Del. February 1865. Exchanged at Boulware & Cox's Wharves, James River, Va., March 10-12, 1865. (Born in Henry County, Ga. November 6, 1842.)

Peebles, John T.- private March 4, 1862. Discharged, disability, August 10, 1862. (Killed in Henry County, Ga. after war.)

Pendley, John M.- private March 4, 1862. Wounded, left arm disabled at Ellison's Mill, Va., June 26, 1862. Discharged on account of wounds at camp near Fredericksburg, Va. December 28, 1862. (Resident of Ga. since November 30, 1841.)

Pendley, William Jasper - private May 5, 1862. Wounded in left arm and right shoulder at Chancellorsville, Va. May 2, 1863. Roll for July - August 1864, last on file, shows him absent, sick. No later record. (Born in Ga. August 29, 1843.)

Phillips, Crawford - private August 22, 1862. Wounded in neck, right arm and chest, and captured at Spotsylvania, Va. May 10, 1864. Died of wounds and pneumonia in Lincoln General Hospital at Washington, D. C. May 29, 1864.

Phillips, David - private March 4, 1862. Died at Richmond, Va. July 12, 1862.

Phillips, James W.- private December 9, 1862. Appears last on roll dated April 1, 1864.

Pierce, William B.- private March 4, 1862. Wounded at Chancellorsville, Va. May 2, 1863. Captured at Spotsylvania, Va. May 10, 1864. Exchanged at Fort Delaware, Del. March 7, 1865. Received at Boulware & Cox's Wharves, James River, Va., March 10-12, 1865.

Price, William C.- private March 4, 1862. Roll for July -August 1864, last on file, shows him present. Captured and paroled at Athens, Ga. May 8, 1865.

Price, W. T.- private. Recruit.

Pullin, Jeptha Polk - private March 4, 1862. Wounded at Spotsylvania, Va. May 10, 1864. Died of wounds.

Rawls, John - private March 4, 1862. Wounded at Sharpsburg, Md. September 17, 1862. Died of wounds and pneumonia in South Carolina Hospital, Post Jefferson at Charlottesville, Va., October 12, 1862. Buried there in Confederate Cemetery.

Rawls, William - private March 4, 1862. Died of disease in General Hospital at Camp Winder at Richmond, Va. September 29, 1862. Buried there in Hollywood Cemetery.

Richardson, Robert B.- private March 4, 1862. Died of pneumonia in General Hospital # 2, at Lynchburg, Va. January 26 or 29, 1863.

Richardson, William M.- private August 22, 1862. Captured at Harper's Ferry, W. Va. July 8, 1864. Released at Elmira, N. Y. May 19, 1865.

Rosser, John A.- private March 4, 1862. Surrendered at Appomattox, Va. April 9, 1865.

Russell, John - private. Recruit. Wounded at Sharpsburg, Md. September 17, 1862. Died of wounds October 11, 1862.

Salter, William - private August 22, 1862. Captured at Spotsylvania, Va. May 10, 1864. Died of smallpox at Fort Delaware, Del. January 1, 1865.

Shaw, James W.- private March 4, 1862. Wounded in 1864. Roll for August 31, 1864, last on file, shows him absent, wound ed. Cemetery records show one J. Shaw was buried in Con federate Cemetery at Spotsylvania, Va.

Shaw, J. M.- private May 5, 1864.

Smith, Joseph J.- private March 4, 1862. Killed at Ellison's Mill, Va. June 26, 1862.

Smith, William Jasper - private March 4, 1862. Transferred to Co. I. Wounded at Spotsylvania, Va. May 10, 1864. Wounded and permanently disabled at Richmond, Va., April 3, 1865. (Born in Morgan County, Ga. March 1839.)

Snidler, Thompson D. T.- See Linder.

Snow, James Marion - private May 5, 1864. Discharged, epilepsy, at Jackson Hospital, Richmond, Va. September 24, 1864. (Born in Gwinnett County, Ga. January 3, 1837.)

Sowell, John Perry - private March 4, 1862. Killed at Ellison's Mill, Va. June 26, 1862.

Sowell, Martin Van Buren - private March 4, 1862. Transferred to Co. F, 53d Regiment Ga. Inf. May 3, 1862. Appointed 3d Sergeant December 1863. Captured at Farmville, Va. April 6, 1865. Released at Newport News, Va. June 15, 1865.

Stancell, John N. (or Stansell) - private March 4, 1862. Killed at Mechanicsville, Va. June 26, 1862.

Stanfield, Abner L.- private February 13, 1863. Roll for August 31, 1864, last on file, shows him sick. No later record.

Stanfield, John H.- private May 5, 1862. Wounded in left thigh at Cedar Creek, Va. October 19, 1864. Admitted to C. S. A. General Hospital at Charlottesville, Va. October 23, 1864. Transferred to Lynchburg, Va. hospital October 25, 1864. Pension records show he was furloughed home November 29, 1864, and was unable to rejoin command. (Born in Henry County, Ga. September 30, 1840.)

Stanfield, William M.- private March 4, 1862. Wounded in head at Gettysburg, Pa. July 1, 1863. Wounded and captured at Spotsylvania, Va. May 10, 1864. Paroled at Fort Delaware, Del. for exchange February 1865. Received at Boulware & Cox's Wharves, James River, Va., March 12, 1865. (Born in Ga. June 25, 1838.)

Street, Francis M.- private March 4, 1862. Discharged, deaf- ness, at camp near Richmond, Va., July 17, 1862.

Tarpley, Henry C.- private December 9, 1862. Captured at High Bridge, Va. April 6, 1865. Released at Newport News, Va. June 26, 1865.

Tarpley, Lucius M.- private March 4, 1862. Died of pneumonia in Richmond, Va. hospital February 1, 1863.

Tarpley, William Hamp - private May 8, 1862. Wounded through hip at Ellison's Mill, Va. June 26, 1862; Chancellorsville, Va. May 2, 1863. Admitted to Chimborazo Hospital #2, at Richmond, Va. June 7, 1863, and furloughed there from for 40 days July 2, 1863. (Born in Ga. May 7, 1832.)

Thompson, Alfred - private March 4, 1862. Transferred from General Hospital #13, at Richmond, Va. to 4th Division General Hospital at Camp Winder, Richmond, Va., September 24, 1862. Returned to duty September 29, 1862. Accidentally killed in service.

Thompson, Wiley - private May 5, 1862. Wounded in right arm at Chancellorsville, Va. May 2, 1863. Medical Examining Board reported him permanently and totally unfit for duty on account of gunshot wound in right wrist, resulting in com pleteanchylosis of joint, March 20, 1865. (Born in Ga. August 11, 1835.)

Turner, Charles - private, March 4, 1862.

Turner, David T.- private March 4, 1862. Roll for August 31, 1864, last on file, shows him present. No later record.

Turner, Hilliard A.- private March 4, 1862. Wounded at South Mountain, Md. September 14, 1862.

Turner, John J.- private March 4, 1862. Wounded at Ellison's Mill, Va. June 26, 1862. Died of wounds in General Hospital #9, at Richmond, Va. July 2, 1862.

Turner, Joseph S.- private. Returned to duty from Jackson Hospital at Richmond, Va. May 21, 1864. No later record.

Turner, M. T.- private April 26, 1864. Surrendered at Appomattox, Va. April 9, 1865. (Born in Henry County, Ga. Died in Spalding County, Ga. December 11, 1912.)

Turner, Peyton S.- private March 4, 1862. Wounded in right leg at Petersburg, Va. March 25, 1865. Admitted to General Hospital at Petersburg, Va., where leg was amputated, March 25, 1865. Captured in hospital April 3, 1865. Died of wounds in Fair Grounds Hospital at Petersburg, Va. May 23 or 28, 1865.

Turnipseed, Jesse C.- private March 4, 1862. Discharged, disability, at camp near Richmond, Va., August 16, 1862.

Turnipseed, John W.- private May 5, 1862. Admitted to Chimborazo Hospital #5, at Richmond, Va. with fever June 25, 1862. Wounded at Chancellorsville, Va. May 3, 1862; Spotsylvania, Va. May 10, 1864. Pension records show he was at home wounded close of war. (Born in Richland District, S. C. July 16, 1843.)

Turnipseed, Nathaniel C.- private March 4, 1862. Wounded in right side at Ellison's Mill, Va. June 26, 1862. Died of wounds between July 3 and 10, 1862.

Upchurch, James M.- private May 1, 1862. Captured at Spotsylvania, Va. May 10, 1864. Paroled at Fort Delaware, Del. February 1865. Exchanged at Boulware & Cox's Wharves, James River, Va., March 10-12, 1865.

Upchurch, Jasper - private March 4, 1862. Wounded, resulting in hernia, in Virginia June 1862. Admitted to Chimborazo Hospital #4, at Richmond, Va. with hernia September 6, 1862. Returned to duty October 9, 1862. Pension records show he was at home on wounded furlough September 25, 1864 -April 1865. (Born in North Carolina October 16, 1830.)

Upchurch, Lloyd A.- private March 4, 1862. Admitted to C. S. A. General Hospital at Charlottesville, Va. October 6, 1862. Returned to duty October 23, 1862.

Weems, Gilbert G.- Enlisted as a private in Co. D, 2d Battn. Ga. Inf. July 1, 1861. Transferred to Co. A, 44th Regiment Ga. Inf. March 4, 1862. Appointed 1st Sergeant May 15, 1862. Wounded, left arm permanently disabled at Fort Steadman, Va., March 25, 1865. Captured in Richmond, Va. hospital April 3, 1865. (Born in Ga. March 31, 1838.)

Weems, James R.- private March 4, 1862. Admitted to Chimborazo Hospital #4, at Richmond, Va. with tonsillitis June 12, 1862. Died of disease June 15, 1862.

Weems, John R.- private March 4, 1862. Killed at Ellison's Mill, Va. June 26, 1862.

Weems, John Walker - Enlisted as a private in Co. D, 2d Battn. Ga. Inf. August 8, 1861. Transferred to Co. A, 44th Regiment Ga. Inf. March 4, 1862. Appointed Sergeant Major July 1862. Wounded and disabled at Chancellorsville, Va. May 2, 1863. Pension records show he was on light duty at Atlanta, Ga. 1863, to close of war. (Born in Ga. December 28, 1842.)

Weems, John Wesley - private March 4, 1862. Wounded, Elli- son's Mill, Va. June 26, 1862.

Wilkins, William J.- private March 4, 1862. Elected Jr. 2d Lieutenant April 1864. Wounded in right arm at Washington, D. C. July 12, 1864. Captured at Amelia Court House, Va. April 4, 1865. Released at Johnson's Island, O. June 20, 1865. (Resident of Ga. since October 4, 1834.)

Williams, James M.- private March 4, 1862. Appointed 3d Corporal in 1862. Wounded at Sharpsburg, Md. September 17, 1862. Appointed 2d Corporal June 1864. Captured at High Bridge, Va. April 6, 1865. Released at Newport News, Va. June 26, 1865.

Wilson, William S. (or William L.) - private March 4, 1862.

Wright, William J.- private March 4, 1862. Discharged, disability, March 1862.

Wyatt, Frank - private March 4, 1862.

Wyatt, George W.- private March 4, 1862. Wounded in neck at Chancellorsville, Va. May 2, 1863. Roll for July -August 1864, last on file, shows him sick. No later record. (Born March 26, 1830.)

GA 44th Infantry Regiment

Company I

This company was also decimated in the war. Like Company A, it too had only 5 men listed at Appomattox.

> 1st Serg't J. M. McClelland,
> Private J. B. Grant,
> Wm. Hooten,
> W. J. Masters,
> W. J. Smith.

This company was originally designated Co. A.

Alliston, Charles W.- Captain March 4, 1862. Killed at Malvern Hill, Va. July 1, 1862.

Smith, Levi J.- 1st Lieutenant March 4, 1862. Captured at Spotsylvania, Va. May 10, 1864. Elected Captain September 19, 1864. Released at Fort Delaware, Del. June 16, 1865. (One of the 600 Confederate Officers exposed to the fire of our guns on Morris Island, S. C.) (Born in Ga. February 17, 1833. Died at Decatur, Ga. April 20, 1900.)

Harris, John H.- 2d Lieutenant March 4, 1862. Elected Captain July 12, 1862. Killed at Winchester, Va. September 19, 1864.

McMullen, Jeremiah A.- Jr. 2d Lieutenant March 4, 1862. Elected 2d Lieutenant July 12, 1862. Captured at Spotsylvania, Va. May 10, 1864. Elected 1st Lieutenant September 19, 1864. Re leased from prison June 16, 1865. (Born in Henry County, Ga. in 1833.)

Jackson, John F.- 1st Sergeant March 4, 1862. Elected Jr. 2d Lieutenant July 12, 1862. Acting Ordnance Officer December 2, 1862. On detached duty, Provost Guard, November 19, 1863 -August 31, 1864. Elected 2d Lieutenant September 19, 1864. Dropped, Spe cial Order #28, February 3, 1865. (Born in Henry County, Ga. January 14, 1830)

McClelland, John F.- 2d Sergeant March 4, 1862. Captured at Spotsylvania, Va. May 10, 1864. Elected Jr. 2d Lieutenant September 19, 1864. Exchanged at Fort Delaware, Del. March 7, 1865. Captured at Richmond, Va. April 3, 1865, and escaped from hospital May 1, 1865.

Streeter, Joseph - 3d Sergeant March 4, 1862. Captured at Spotsylvania, Va. May 10, 1864. Paroled at Fort Delaware, Del. February 1865, and exchanged there March 7, 1865. Received at Boulware & Cox's

Wharves, James River, Va., March 10-12, 1865. Died on steamer en route home in 1865. Buried at Aiken's Landing, Va.

Bryans, Greenberry S.- 4th Sergeant March 4, 1862. Captured at Spotsylvania, Va. May 10, 1864. Died of smallpox at Fort Delaware, Del. February 8, 1865.

Shaw, Eugenius N.- Enlisted as a private in Co. G, Cobb's Legion Ga. Inf. July 29, 1861. Discharged November 27, or 30, 1861. Appointed 5th Sergeant of Co. I, 44th Regiment Ga. Inf. March 4, 1862. Roll for July -August 1864, last on file, shows him present. Killed at Spotsylvania, Va. May 12, 1864 or at Fisher's Hill, Va. September 22, 1864.

Almand, William A.- 1st Corporal March 4, 1862.

Bryans, Bluford H.- 2d Corporal March 4, 1862. Appointed 1st Corporal. Wounded at Fisher's Hill, Va. September 22, 1864. Died from wounds in 1864.

Lemon, Abraham - 3d Corporal March 4, 1862. Appointed Sergeant. Captured at Petersburg, Va. April 2, 1865. Released at Point Lookout, Md. June 29, 1865.

Fargerson, Roderick H.- 4th Corporal March 4, 1862. Discharged on account of defective vision, at camp near Richmond, Va., July 14, 1862.

Allen, J. N.- private March 4, 1862.

Ashmore, William P.- private March 4, 1862. Appointed Corporal. Died of disease in Henry County, Ga. February 5, 1864.

Atkinson, James C.- private March 4, 1862. Captured at Spotsylvania, Va. May 10, 1864. Paroled at Fort Delaware, Del. February 1865. Received at Boulware & Cox's Wharves, James

River, Va. for exchange, March 10-12, 1865. Admitted to Jack- son Hospital at Richmond, Va. with diarrhea March 11, 1865. Died March 27, 1865. Buried in Hollywood Cemetery at Richmond, Va.

Backus, Edmund O.- private March 4, 1862. Captured at Spotsylvania, Va. May 10, 1864. Paroled at Fort Delaware, Del. February 1865. Received at Boulware & Cox's Wharves, James

River, Va. for exchange, March 10-12, 1865.

Bailey, David H.- private March 4, 1862. Killed at Ellison's Mill, Va. June 26, 1862.

Barnes, Columbus M.- private May 15, 1862. Captured at Wilderness, Va. May 5, 1864. Died of variola at Elmira, N. Y. February 17, 1865. Grave #2197, Woodlawn National Cemetery.

Barnes, Cornelius W.- private March 25, 1864. Detailed at Staunton, Va. June 1864. Roll dated August 31, 1864, last on file, shows him present. No later record.

Barnes, William H.- private March 4, 1862.

Beasley, William W. Y.- private March 4, 1862. Appointed Regimental Fifer May 1, 1863. Roll dated August 31, 1864, last on file, shows him present. Pension records show he surrendered at Appomattox, Va. April 9, 1865. (Born in Abbeville County, S. C. March 18, 1826.)

Bentley, Isaiah T. M.- private March 4, 1862. Appointed 4th Corporal in 1862. Severely wounded at Fredericksburg, Va. December 13, 1862. Captured near Spotsylvania, Va. May 10, 1864. Paroled at Fort Delaware, Del. February 1865. Received at James River, Va. May 12, 1865.

Bevin, Robert M. (or Bivins) - private March 4, 1862. Admitted to Jackson Hospital at Richmond, Va. June 2, 1864. Returned to duty September 19, 1864. Pension records show he was at home on sick furlough close of war. (Born in Lincoln County, Ga. in 1825.)

Brewer, George A.- private March 4, 1862. Wounded at Elli- son's Mill, Va. June 26, 1862.

Brooks, James W.- private May 9, 1862. Captured at Spotsyl- vania, Va. May 10, 1864. Paroled at Fort Delaware, Del. February 1865. Received at Boulware & Cox's Wharves, James River,

Va. for exchange, March 10-12, 1865. Died on steamship in route home. Buried at Aiken's Landing, James River, Va.

Brooks, William A.- private April 14, 1864. Captured at Fisher's Hill, Va. September 22, 1864. Paroled at Point Lookout, Md. and received at Boulware & Cox's Wharves, James River, Va. for exchange, March 19, 1865.

Brown, D. Coleman Patrick - private March 4, 1862. Discharged on account of chronic cystitis, at camp near Grace Church, Va., April 20, 1863.

Brown, William (Dr.) - private March 4, 1862. Discharged in 1862.

Brown, William B.- private March 4, 1862. Captured at Spot- sylvania, Va. May 10, 1864. Transferred to

Aiken's Landing, Va. for exchange September 30, 1864. No later record.

Bryant, David - private March 4, 1862. Died in Richmond, Va. hospital.

Butler, John C.- private March 4, 1862. Died of disease in Hos- pital #17, August 20, 1862.

Butler, Warren Hubbard - private May 15, 1862. Wounded at Ellison's Mill, Va. June 26, 1862. Captured at Spotsylvania, Va. May 10, 1864. Paroled at Fort Delaware, Del. and ex changed there March 7, 1865. (Born in Greene County, Ga. October 14, 1826.)

Campbell, Robert C.- private March 4, 1862. Wounded in eye, resulting in loss of sight. Died of disease at Madison, Ga. January 11, 1864.

Cannon, Charles S.- private March 4, 1862. Died of disease at Orange Court House, Va. August 4, 1863.

Cannon, Edward Lewis P.- private March 4, 1862. Died of disease in Richmond, Va. hospital April 14, 1863.

Carroll, Benjamin F. (Jack) - private March 4, 1862. Killed at Guinea Station, Va. December 14, 1862.

Chaffin, Robert C.- private May 15, 1862. Wounded at Elli- son's Mill, Va. June 26, 1862. Captured at Spotsylvania, Va. May 10, 1864. Died of chronic diarrhea at Fort Delaware, Del. March 1, 1865.

Cheney, George F.- private May 6, 1862. Captured at Spotsylvania, Va. May 10, 1864. Paroled at Fort Delaware, Del. February 1865. Received at Boulware & Cox's Wharves, James River, Va. for exchange, March 10-12, 1865. (Born in Ga. in 1844.)

Clack, James J.- private March 4, 1862. Captured at Spotsylvania, Va. May 10, 1864. Exchanged at Fort Delaware, Del. March 7, 1865.

Clark, William P.- private March 6, 1862. Captured at Spotsylvania, Va. May 10, 1864. Sent to Fort Delaware, Del. May 21, 1864. Paroled February 1865, and exchanged there March 7, 1865.

Clifton, William L.- private May 15, 1862. Captured at Spotsylvania, Va. May 10, 1864. Sent to Fort Delaware, Del. May 21, 1864, paroled February 1865, and exchanged there March 7, 1865.

Cook, Columbus M.- private March 4, 1862. Wounded at Elli- son's Mill, Va. June 26, 1.862. Admitted to General Hospital at Howard's Grove, Richmond, Va. in 1862. Transferred to Ban ner

Hospital July 14, 1862. Died from wounds in DeKalb County, Ga. March 30, 1863.

Cook, Elijah - private March 4, 1862. Captured at Spotsylvania, Va. May 10, 1864. Sent to Fort Delaware, Del. May 21, 1864, and died there October 25, 1864.

Cook, Harper - private March 4, 1862.

Cook, John W.- private March 4, 1862. Captured at Spotsyl- vania, Va. May 10, 1864. Sent to Fort Delaware, Del. May 21, 1864, and died there from inflammation of brain, October 24, 1864.

Cook, William M.- private March 4, 1862. Captured at Spotsyl- vania, Va. May 10, 1864. Sent to Fort Delaware, Del. May 21, 1864, and died there of smallpox February 16, 1865.

Duke, John G.- private March 4, 1862. Wounded at Winches- ter, Va. September 19, 1864.

Dulin, John C., Jr.- private March 4, 1862. Wounded and dis- abled at Ellison's Mill, Va. June 26, 1862. Roll dated August 31, 1864, last on file, shows he was detached as shoemaker at At lanta, Ga. April 14, 1863. Remained on detail until close of war. Paroled at Augusta, Ga. May 1, 1865. (Born February 1, 1837.)

Fears, James P.- private March 4, 1862. Admitted to Chimbo- razo Hospital #4, at Richmond, Va., July 7, 1862. Returned to duty September 1, 1862. Discharged, under-age.

Few, Elisha - private March 4, 1862. Discharged on account of defective vision, at Camp McIntosh near Goldsboro, N. C., May 15, 1862.

Ford, James W.- private May 6, 1862. Wounded at Ellison's Mill, Va. June 26, 1862. Died of typhoid fever in General Hos pital at Camp Winder, Richmond, Va., September 2, 1862. Buried there in Hollywood Cemetery.

Ford, Marcus D.- private March 4, 1862. Admitted to Hospital #4, at Richmond, Va. June 12, 1862. Discharged on account of disabled arm and hand in 1862. (Born April 18, 1833. Died May 24, 1913.)

Friday, Daniel H. (or Frida) - private in 1862. Killed at Chan- cellorsville, Va. May 2, 1863.

Fuller, George W.- private March 4, 1862. Killed at Ellison's Mill, Va. June 26, 1862.

George, Jesse N.- private March 4, 1862. Roll dated August 31, 1864, last on file, shows him absent, detailed for hospital duty at Wilson, N. C. January 22, 1864. No later record.

Gill, J. J.- private March 4, 1862. Transferred to Co. A, 54th Regiment Ga. Inf. in 1864. Pension records show he surrendered at Greensboro, N. C. April 26, 1865. (Born in Meriwether County, Ga.)

Grant, Joseph B.- private March 4, 1862. Wounded at Ellison's Mill, Va. June 26, 1862. Surrendered at Appomattox, Va. April 9, 1865. (Born in Ga.)

Gunn, Willis R.- private March 4, 1862. Admitted to Richmond, Va. hospital with rheumatism July 3, 1862. Returned to duty August 7, 1862. No later record.

Hanson, J. Newton - private March 4, 1862. Died of pneumonia in Richmond, Va. hospital January 4, 1863.

Hanson, Robert, Jr.- private March 4, 1862. Discharged on ac- count of epilepsy, at Camp McIntosh near Goldsboro, N. C., May 6, 1862.

Harkness, Elias A.- private March 4, 1862. Admitted to C.S.A. Hospital at Charlottesville, Va. with diarrhoea January 4, 1864. Returned to duty January 16, 1864. Roll dated August 31, 1864, last on file, shows him present. Pension records show he was cap tured and paroled in Virginia April 1865. (Born in Butts Coun ty, Ga. December 1833.)

Harkness, John L.- private March 4, 1862. Wounded at Elli- son's Mill, Va. June 26, 1862. Admitted to General Hospital at Richmond, Va. June 27, 1862. Furloughed for 30 days July 7, 1862. Wounded on picket line and died at Kelly's Ford, Va. November 7, 1863.

Harper, Cordy T.- private August 16, 1862. Captured near Petersburg, Va. March 25, 1865. Released at Point Lookout, Md. June 13, 1865. (Born in Ga.)

Harper, Thomas J.- private March 4, 1862. Captured at Spotsyl- vania, Va. May 10, 1864. Released at Fort Delaware, Del. June 16, 1865. (Born in Madison County, Ga. April 3, 1840.)

Hearn, Benjamin F. (Tobe) - private March 4, 1862. Dis- charged, disability, July 31, 1863. Enlisted as a private in Co. H, 27th Regiment Ga. Inf. June 1864. Wounded in head, date and place not given. Captured in 1865. Released at Fort Delaware, Del. in 1865. (Born in Henry County, Ga. April 25, 1841.)

Hester, Francis M.- private March 4, 1862. Wounded and cap- tured at Winchester, Va. September 19, 1864. Paroled at Point Lookout, Md. and transferred to

Aiken's Landing, Va. for ex change March 15, 1865. (Born in Newton County, Ga. in 1848. Died at Williston, Fla. in 1912.)

Hogan, Andrew J.- private March 4, 1862. Captured at Spot- sylvania, Va. May 10, 1864. Paroled at Fort Delaware, Del. February 1865.

Hollis, John - private March 4, 1862. Died of typhoid pneu- monia at Orange Court House, Va. March 1, 1864.

Hooten, John G.- private March 4, 1862. Admitted to General Hospital #l4, in 1862. Returned to duty December 3, 1862. Wound ed at Winchester, Va. September 19, 1864. Died from wounds.

Hooten, William A.- private March 4, 1862. Admitted to Gen- eral Hospital #14, at Farmville, Va. with rheumatism, September 5, 1862. Returned to duty October 15, 1862. Discharged December 4, 1862. Reenlisted March 11, 1864. Wounded June 1864. At home, wounded, August 31, 1864. Wounded at Fisher's Hill, Va. September 22, 1864. Surrendered at Appomattox, Va. April 9, 1865. (Born in Henry County, Ga. April 22, 1846.)

Hubbard, Mathew White - private March 4, 1862. Captured at Spotsylvania, Va. May 10, 1864. Paroled at Fort Delaware, Del. February 1865, and exchanged there March 7, 1865. Received at Boulware & Cox's Wharves, James River, Va., March 10-12, 1865. (Born in Jasper County, Ga. in 1837.)

Hunt, Jerry M.- private March 4, 1862. Wounded at Ellison's Mill, Va. June 26, 1862. Died of wounds in St. Charles Hos pital at Richmond, Va. August 24, 1862.

Hunt, John H.- private January 11, 1864. Captured at Spotsyl- vania, Va. May 10, 1864. Released at Fort Delaware, Del. June 16, 1865. (Born in Henry County, Ga. in 1846.)

Jackson, John Alford - private July 24, 1862. Captured at Spotsylvania, Va. May 10, 1864. Paroled at Fort Delaware, Del. and transferred to Aiken's Landing, Va. for exchange September 30, 1864. Received at Varina, Va. October 5, 1864. No later record. (Died in Henry County, Ga. January 21, 1917.)

Jackson, Peter W.- private August 8, 1862. Captured at Spotsylvania, Va. May 10, 1864. Paroled at Fort Delaware, Del. February 1865. Exchanged there March 7, 1865. Received at Boulware & Cox's Wharves, James River, Va., March 10-12, 1865. Admitted to General Hospital #9, at Richmond, Va., March 12, 1865. Furloughed for 30 days March 14, 1865.

Jackson, Roderick W.- See Co. A.

James, Josiah M. (or Josiah W.) - private March 4, 1862. Wounded at Guinea Station, Va. December 14, 1862. Died from wounds in General Hospital #14, at Richmond, Va. January 2, 1863.

Johnson, William A.- See private Co. D.

Keene, George B.- private March 4, 1862. Wounded April 1864. Captured at Spotsylvania, Va. May 10, 1864. Paroled at Fort Delaware, Del. February 1865, and exchanged there March 7, 1865. Admitted to Jackson Hospital at Richmond, Va. with chronic diarrhoea March 13, 1865.

Kelley, Thomas H.- private March 4, 1862. Captured at Spot- sylvania, Va. May 10, 1864. Paroled at Fort Delaware, Del. February 1865. Received at Boulware & Cox's Wharves, James

River, Va., March 10-12, 1865. Pension records show he died of disease in Fort Delaware, Del. prison February 25, 1865.

Kimble, J. G.- private March 4, 1862. Died at Richmond, Va. May 8, 1862. Buried there in Hollywood Cemetery.

Knight, James B.- private March 4, 1862. Admitted to C.S.A. General Hospital at Charlottesville, Va. with diarrhoea July 22, 1864. Transferred to Lynchburg, Va. September 26, 1864. Ad mitted to C.S.A. General Hospital at Charlottesville, Va. October 24, 1864, and died there of pneumonia October 27, 1864.

Langford, James M.- private March 4, 1862. Admitted to Chimborazo Hospital #4, at Richmond, Va., with chronic diarrhoea and bronchitis, June 24, 1862. Admitted to General Hospital at Camp Winder, Richmond, Va. April 4, 1863, and furloughed for 30 days April 5, 1863. Died of disease in Henry County, Ga., while home on sick furlough.

Leon, Morris - private March 4, 1862. Captured at Spotsylvania, Va. May 10, 1864. Took oath of allegiance to U.S. Govt. at Fort Delaware, Del. and released February 13, 1865.

Lewis, John W.- private March 4, 1862. Died of pneumonia August 7, 1862. Buried in Confederate Cemetery at Lynchburg, Va. No. 7, 4th Line, Lot 162 - Warwick House.

Lewis, William Henry - private March 4, 1862. Appointed 3d Corporal in 1862. Wounded in hip and captured at Spotsylvania, Va. May 10, 1864. Paroled at

Fort Delaware, Del. February 1865. Exchanged March 7, 1865. (Born in Morgan County, Ga. in 1824.)

Lewis, William P.- private March 4, 1862. Died of chronic diarrhea in General Hospital #16, at Richmond, Va. October 7, 1862. 824

Mann, William G.- private May 6, 1862. Wounded, date and place not given. Died of disease at Orange Court House, Va. January 26, 1864.

Martin, J. H.- private March 4, 1862. Died at Richmond, Va. June 3, 1862. Buried there in Hollywood Cemetery.

Masters, William J.- private March 4, 1862. Surrendered at Appomattox, Va. April 9, 1865.

Mathews, R. B. (or Osborn S.) - private May 15, 1862. Cap- tured at Spotsylvania, Va. May 10, 1864. Died from abscessed hip at Fort Delaware, Del. February 2, 1865.

Mathews, William O.- private March 4, 1862. Died of disease August 4, 1862.

McCarthy, James - private March 4, 1862. Discharged, disabil- ity, at Camp Ripley July 28, 1862. Died of disease in 1862.

McClelland, James M.- Enlisted as a private in Co. D, 3d Battn. Ga. State Troops November 18, 1861. Roll dated April 17, 1862, last on file, shows him present. Mustered out in 1862. Enlisted as a private in Co. I, 44th Regiment Ga. Inf. May 6, 1862. Appointed Quartermaster Sergeant May 6, 1863. Appointed 1st Sergeant and returned to company. Surrendered at Appomattox, Va. April 9, 1865.

McClelland, William R.- Enlisted as a private in Co. D, 3d Battn. Ga. State Troops November 18, 1861. Roll for April 17, 1862, last on file, shows him present. Mustered out in 1862. Enlisted as a private in Co. I, 44th Regiment Ga. Inf. May 6, 1862. Wounded at Spotsylvania, Va. May 10, 1864. Died from wounds.

McCoy, William T.- private March 4, 1862. Captured at Waynesboro, Pa. July 6, 1863. Paroled at Baltimore, Md. August 23, 1863. Received at City Point, Va. for exchange August 24, 1863. No later record.

McElroy, Jesse - private March 4, 1862.

McMullen, Sanford W.- private March 4, 1862. Wounded at Ellison's Mill, Va. June 26, 1862. Died of wounds in 2d Ga. Hospital at Richmond, Va. June 30, 1862.

Morgan, Jesse M.- private March 4, 1862. Discharged.

First Families of McDonough & Henry County 189

Morris, Joseph T.- private March 4, 1862. Wounded at Elli- son's Mill, Va. June 26, 1862. Died of wounds July 4, 1862.

Morris, Robert Newton - private March 4, 1862. Wounded, date and place not given. Died from wounds.

Morton, William J.- private March 4, 1862.

Moss, William J.- Enlisted as a private in Co. D, 3d Battalion Ga. State Troops December 11, 1861. Roll dated April 17, 1862, last on file, shows him present. Mustered out in 1862. Enlisted as a private in Co. I, 44th Regiment Ga. Inf. in 1862. Appointed 1st Sergeant. Wounded through throat and permanently disabled at Wilderness, Va. May 5, 1864. Furloughed by Medical Examining Board at Augusta, Ga. February 1, 1865. Recommended for extension of 30 days March 31, 1865. (Born in Ga.)

Murray, George T.- private April 11, 1864. Captured at Spotsylvania, Va. May 10, 1864. Paroled at Fort Delaware, Del. March 7, 1865. Received at Boulware & Cox's Wharves, James

River, Va. for exchange, March 10-12, 1865. Captured and paroled at Athens, Ga. May 8, 1865. (Born in Ga. in 1844.)

Murray, James M.- private March 4, 1862. Captured at Spotsylvania, Va. May 10, 1864. Paroled at Fort Delaware, Del. February 1865. Received at Boulware & Cox's Wharves, James

River, Va. for exchange, March 10-12, 1865.

Orr, Noah - private March 4, 1862. Died of disease in service.

Paschal, Richard H. C.- See private Co. F.

Pattillo, Silas L.- private May 15, 1862. Captured at Spotsyl- vania, Va. May 10, 1864. Paroled at Fort Delaware, Del. February 1863. Received at Boulware & Cox's Wharves, James River, Va. for exchange, March 10-12, 1865.

Perryman, Freeman W.- private March 4, 1862. Died at Madison, Ga., while home on sick furlough, September 8, 1862.

Powell, James T.- private May 4, 1862. Captured at Fort Gregg, Va. April 2, 1865. Released at Point Lookout, Md. June 17, 1865.

Reeves, Abner - private March 4, 1862. Wounded at Ellison's Mill, Va. June 26, 1862. Died of wounds in Richmond, Va. hospital July 17, 1862.

Riley, James M.- private March 4, 1862. Wounded and disabled April 1864. In hospital, wounded, August 31, 1864. In hospital as guard January 21, 1865. No later record.

Roberts, David O.- private March 4, 1862. Captured at Spotsylvania, Va. May 10, 1864. Paroled at Fort Delaware, Del. February 1865, and exchanged there March 7, 1865. Admitted to General Hospital #9, at Richmond, Va., March 10, 1865; sent to Jackson Hospital there March 11, 1865.

Roberts, William H.- private May 1, 1862. Captured at High Bridge, Va. April 6, 1865. Released at Newport News, Va. June 15, 1865.

Robertson, Alonzo G.- private March 4, 1862. Died of disease in General Hospital #16, at Richmond, Va. September 18, 1862.

Robertson, Wilson L.- private March 4, 1862. Died of disease in Madison, Ga. hospital, while home on sick furlough, June 25, 1864.

Rowland, Berry (or Roland) - private March 4, 1862.

Sappington, James H.- private March 4, 1862. Captured at Spotsylvania, Va. May 10, 1864. Died of smallpox at Fort Delaware, Del. January 1, 1865.

Sappington, John T.- private March 4, 1862. Died of measles near Richmond, Va. June 30, 1862.

Smith, Ferdinand R. (or Fernanders R.) - private March 4, 1862. 826

Captured at Spotsylvania, Va. May 10, 1864. Exchanged at Fort Delaware, Del. March 7, 1865. Received at Boulware & Cox's Wharves, James River, Va., March 10-12, 1865.

Smith, James M.- private March 4, 1862. Pension records show he was sick in hospital close of war. Paroled at Greensboro, N. C. April 26, 1865. (Born in Morgan County, Ga. about 1824 or 1825.)

Smith, William Jasper - See Co. A.

South, Francis C.- private May 16, 1862. Killed at Ellison's Mill, Va. June 26, 1862.

South, Newton M.- private March 4, 1862. Wounded at Ellison's Mill, Va. June 26, 1862. Captured at Spotsylvania, Va. May 10, 1864. Paroled at Fort Delaware, Del. February 1866. Ex changed March 7, 1865. Received at Boulware & Cox's Wharves, James River, Va., March 10-12, 1865.

Stanton, John H.- private March 4, 1862. Discharged, furnished substitute, in 1862.

Stapp, Henry J.- private March 4, 1862. Died in Depot Hospital at Guinea Station, Va. January 31, 1863.

Stapp, Solomon J.- private March 4, 1862. Roll dated August 31, 1864, last on file, shows him present, detailed Provost Guard November 15, 1862. No later record. (Born in Ga.)

Stapp, Thomas W. J.- private May 15, 1862. Wounded in right leg, body, and left arm, at Chancellorsville, Va. May 2, 1868; at Spotsylvania, Va. May 10, 1864. Roll dated August 31, 1864, last on file, shows him absent in hospital, wounded. (Born April 24, 1833.)

Stark, Thomas P. J.- private March 4, 1862. Admitted to General Hospital #18, at Richmond, Va. with fever, July 14, and died July 19, 1862.

Tomlin, A. J.- private in 1862. Admitted to Winder Hospital, Division #3, at Richmond, Va., December 1, 1862. Transferred to Danville, Va. December 27, 1862. No later record.

Tomlin, Milton L.- private March 4, 1862. Killed at Ellison's Mill, Va. June 26, 1862.

Tomlin, Newton J.- private May 17, 1862. Died of pneumonia at Gordonsville, Va. March 23, 1863.

Walker, Rufus John - private May 15, 1862. In hospital October 10, 1862. Died of measles at Richmond; Va. in 1862.

White, David T.- private March 4, 1862. Killed at Ellison's Mill, Va. June 26, 1862.

Whooten, William A.- See Hooten, William A.

Winfrey, Thomas E.- private March 4, 1862. Wounded at Ellison's Mill, Va. June 26, 1862. Admitted to General Hospital at Howard's Grove, Richmond, Va., severely wounded in left thigh, June 27, 1862. Died from wounds July 16, 1862.

Wood, John W.- private March 4, 1862. Discharged, furnished substitute, June 20, 1862. 827

Woods, Winchester - private March 4, 1862. Died from brain fever at Richmond, Va. in 1862.

Youngblood, Cincinnatus - private March 4, 1862. Sick in hospital August 31, 1864. Captured at Fort Gregg, Va. April 2, 1865. Released at Point Lookout, Md. June 22, 1865.

Zachry, Clementius R.- private March 4, 1862. Pension records show he left command in Virginia on 60 days' furlough November 1864, unable to return. (Born in Ga. in 1840.)

Index

Brooks, William A. ~ 44INF-I
Brown, D. Coleman Patrick ~ 44INF-I
Brown, Loren S. ~ 22INF-K
Brown, Warren J. ~ 19INF-G
Brown, William (Dr.) ~ 44INF-I
Brown, William B. ~ 44INF-I
Bryans, Bluford H. ~ 44INF-I
Bryans, Greenberry S. ~ 44INF-I
Bryant, David ~ 44INF-I
Bunn, G. W. ~ 44INF-A
Bunn, Joseph L. ~ 44INF-A
Bunn, William ~ 19INF-G
Butler, John C. ~ 44INF-I
Butler, Warren Hubbard ~ 44INF-I
Cagle, David ~ 44INF-A
Cagle, William W. ~ 44INF-A
Callaway, Isaac W. ~ 22INF-K
Callaway, James Sandford ~ 44INF-A
Callaway, John A. ~ 22INF-K
Callaway, Jonathan Burton ~ 44INF-A
Camp, Aaron N. ~ 44INF-A
Campbell, Robert C. ~ 44INF-I
Cannon, Charles S. ~ 44INF-I
Cannon, Edward Lewis P. ~ 44INF-I
Carmichael, James C. ~ 44INF-A
Carmichael, John R. ~ 19INF-G
Carmichael, Samuel H. ~ 44INF-A

Carroll, Benjamin F. (Jack) ~ 44INF-I
Carroll, Columbus C. ~ 22INF-K
Carroll, John H. ~ 22INF-K
Carroll, Josiah D. ~ 22INF-K
Carroll, Needham J. ~ 22INF-K
Carroll, Richmond T. ~ 22INF-K
Carroll, William A. ~ 22INF-K
Carroll, William Anson ~ 19INF-G
Chaffin, Robert C. ~ 44INF-I
Cheney, George F. ~ 44INF-I
Clack, James J. ~ 44INF-I
Clark, William P. ~ 44INF-I
Clarke, Amos J. ~ 22INF-K
Clarke, David ~ 22INF-K
Clarke, Henry W. ~ 22INF-K
Clarke, Thomas A. ~ 22INF-K
Clarke, Warren J. ~ 22INF-K
Clay, Henry J. ~ 22INF-K
Clayton, Francis M. ~ 22INF-K
Clifton, William L. ~ 44INF-I
Cloud, Cullen ~ 44INF-A
Coe, James N. ~ 22INF-K
Cole, Clem C. ~ 19INF-G
Connally, George W. ~ 19INF-G
Cook, Benjamin F. ~ 19INF-G
Cook, Columbus M. ~ 44INF-I
Cook, Elijah ~ 44INF-I
Cook, Harper ~ 44INF-I
Cook, Jabez F. ~ 19INF-G
Cook, John B. ~ 22INF-K
Cook, John W. ~ 44INF-I

Cook, William M. ~ 44INF-I
Cook, William N. ~ 19INF-G
Cooper, Jarratt T. (or Jarrett T.) ~ 44INF-A
Crabbe, George H. ~ 19INF-G
Crabbe, William J. ~ 19INF-G
Crane, Samuel S. ~ 22INF-K
Credille, Cullen G. ~ 44INF-A
Credille, Henry M. ~ 44INF-A
Credille, James M. ~ 44INF-A
Credille, Josiah P. ~ 44INF-A
Daniel, Cicero H. ~ 44INF-A
Daniel, Henry A. ~ 44INF-A
Darsey, George M. T. ~ 44INF-A
Darsey, John T. ~ 44INF-A
Deal, Marcellus R. ~ 22INF-K
Deas, Daniel B. ~ 44INF-A
Deas, Henry T. ~ 44INF-A
Deas, Simeon Asberry ~ 44INF-A
Derrick (Derick), Wallace J. ~ 44INF-A
Derrick, James Wyatt ~ 44INF-A
Derrick, John G. ~ 44INF-A
Derrick, Thomas S. ~ 44INF-A
Derrick, William D. ~ 44INF-A
Dodson, Felix F. ~ 22INF-K
Dodson, George W. ~ 22INF-K
Doyal, William T. ~ 22INF-K
Driver, Charles ~ 44INF-A
Duke, John G. ~ 44INF-I
Dulin, John C. (or Doolin) ~ 44INF-A
Dulin, John C., Jr. ~ 44INF-I
Duncan, Henry M. ~ 22INF-K
Elliott, Baylor S. ~ 19INF-G
Elliott, George, T. ~ 19INF-G
Elliott, Henry S. ~ 19INF-G
Elliott, Hiram T. ~ 19INF-G
Elliott, John Joseph ~ 19INF-G
Elliott, John R. ~ 19INF-G
Elliott, Septimus Adolphus ~ 19INF-G
Elliott, Thomas S. ~ 19INF-G
English, John R. ~ 19INF-G
Fargerson, Roderick H. ~ 44INF-I
Farmer, Charles ~ 44INF-A
Farmer, William H. ~ 44INF-A
Farris, Joel H. ~ 19INF-G
Fears, James P. ~ 44INF-I
Few, Elisha ~ 44INF-I
Fields, Amaziah H. ~ 44INF-A
Fisher, James M. ~ 19INF-G
Fitzgerald, Patrick ~ 22INF-K
Flynt, Tilghman W. ~ 19INF-G
Ford, James W. ~ 44INF-I
Ford, Marcus D. ~ 44INF-I
Ford, Napoleon E. ~ 22INF-K
Friday, Daniel H. (or Frida) ~ 44INF-I
Fuller, George W. ~ 44INF-I
Gardner, Pitts J. ~ 19INF-G
Gardner, William A. ~ 22INF-K
Gay, Jacob ~ 44INF-A
George A. H. ~ 22INF-K
George, David ~ 22INF-K
George, Jesse N. ~ 44INF-I
George, Levi J. ~ 22INF-K
George, Russell A. ~ 22INF-K

Gibson, Harrison ~ 44INF-A
Gibson, James ~ 44INF-A
Gibson, Patrick ~ 44INF-A
Gice, Joseph ~ 44INF-A
Gill, J. J. ~ 44INF-I
Gleaton, George W.(or Gladen) ~ 19INF-G
Gosden, Frank W ~ 19INF-G
Gosden, James (or Gosdin) ~ 19INF-G
Gosden, William F.(or Gosdin) ~ 19INF-G
Goss, Eaby. See Goss, Yerby A. ~ 44INF-A
Goss, Thomas Monroe ~ 44INF-A
Goss, Yerby A. ~ 44INF-A
Grant, Benjamin F. ~ 44INF-A
Grant, Benjamin W. ~ 19INF-G
Grant, Isaac A. ~ 19INF-G
Grant, Isaac M. ~ 22INF-K
Grant, John ~ 19INF-G
Grant, Joseph B. ~ 44INF-I
Grant, Reuben J. ~ 22INF-K
Grant, William M. ~ 22INF-K
Gray, J. A. ~ 19INF-G
Gray, Jonathan S. ~ 19INF-G
Gray, Nelson ~ 19INF-G
Gray, Oliver S. ~ 19INF-G
Gray, Thomas J. ~ 44INF-A
Green, Crawford ~ 44INF-A
Green, Henry F. ~ 22INF-K
Green, Samuel Patterson ~ 22INF-K
Green, William A. ~ 22INF-K
Guest, James M. ~ 19INF-G
Gunn, Willis R. ~ 44INF-I

Hambrick, John B. ~ 19INF-G
Hand, James ~ 19INF-G
Hand, James Henderson ~ 44INF-A
Hand, Johnson ~ 19INF-G
Hand, Thomas H. ~ 19INF-G
Hanson, J. Newton ~ 44INF-I
Hanson, Robert, Jr. ~ 44INF-I
Hardegree, Hiram ~ 44INF-A
Hardin, James L ~ 22INF-K
Harkness, Elias A. ~ 44INF-I
Harkness, John L. ~ 44INF-I
Harper, Cordy T. ~ 44INF-I
Harper, Henry ~ 19INF-G
Harper, John ~ 19INF-G
Harper, Robert H. ~ 19INF-G
Harper, Roderick Henry ~ 44INF-A
Harper, T. L. (or T. S.) ~ 19INF-G
Harper, Thomas ~ 19INF-G
Harper, Thomas J. ~ 44INF-I
Harris, James E. ~ 44INF-A
Harris, John H. ~ 44INF-I
Hearn, Benjamin F. (Tobe) ~ 44INF-I
Helms, John A. ~ 22INF-K
Henry, E. Z. ~ 22INF-K
Henry, Reuben H. ~ 44INF-A
Hester, Francis M. ~ 44INF-I
Hinton,William J.(or W. T.) ~ 22INF-K
Hogan, Andrew J. ~ 44INF-I
Hollis, John ~ 44INF-I
Hooks, Martin V. ~ 22INF-K
Hooten, Cosby A. ~ 19INF-G
Hooten, John G. ~ 44INF-I
Hooten, William A. ~ 44INF-I

Hopkins, Hugh E. ~ 44INF-A
Howell, James ~ 22INF-K
Hubbard, Marshall C. ~ 44INF-A
Hubbard, Mathew White ~ 44INF-I
Hunt, Jerry M. ~ 44INF-I
Hunt, John H. ~ 44INF-I
Jackson, Edmund E. ~ 44INF-A
Jackson, John Alford ~ 44INF-I
Jackson, John F. ~ 44INF-I
Jackson, John R. ~ 44INF-A
Jackson, Marcus L. C. ~ 19INF-G
Jackson, Peter W. ~ 44INF-I
Jackson, Roderick W. ~ 44INF-A
Jackson, Roderick W. ~ 44INF-I
Jackson, Sandford ~ 44INF-A
James, Josiah M. (or Josiah W.) ~ 44INF-I
Jarrett, J. H. ~ 44INF-A
Jarrett, William J. (or William T.) ~ 44INF-A
Jenkins, John H. ~ 44INF-A
Johnson, George Allen ~ 19INF-G
Johnson, James A. ~ 19INF-G
Johnson, James C. ~ 22INF-K
Johnson, James M. ~ 19INF-G
Johnson, Jesse James ~ 19INF-G
Johnson, John C. ~ 22INF-K
Johnson, Luke ~ 19INF-G
Johnson, Thomas D. F. ~ 44INF-A
Johnson, William A. ~ 44INF-I
Johnson, William R. ~ 19INF-G
Joiner, Seaborn Bennett W. ~ 44INF-A
Jones, John M. ~ 44INF-A
Jones, William ~ 44INF-A
Juice, Joseph ~ 44INF-A
Keene, George B. ~ 44INF-I
Kelley, Henry H. (or Kelly) ~ 19INF-G
Kelley, John M. (or Kelly) ~ 19INF-G
Kelley, Joseph T. (or Kelly) ~ 19INF-G
Kelley, Thomas H. ~ 44INF-I
Kelly, Thomas ~ 22INF-K
Kimbell, John K. ~ 44INF-A
Kimble, J. G. ~ 44INF-I
Kitchens, Thomas J. ~ 22INF-K
Knight, James B. ~ 44INF-I
Langford, James M. ~ 44INF-I
Lemon, Abraham ~ 44INF-I
Leon, Morris ~ 44INF-I
Lewis, John W. ~ 44INF-I
Lewis, Lewis ~ 19INF-G
Lewis, William Henry ~ 44INF-I
Lewis, William P. ~ 44INF-I
Linder, Thompson D. T. ~ 44INF-A
Little, Adam E. ~ 44INF-A
Little, Demosthenes C. ~ 44INF-A

Little, Zabud M. ~ 44INF-A

Livingston, L. M. ~ 22INF-K

Livingston, Loren B. ~ 22INF-K

Love, Mark J. ~ 19INF-G

Lowe, James P. ~ 22INF-K

Lowery, George L. ~ 44INF-A

Lowery, Jackson ~ 44INF-A

Maddox, Jacob ~ 19INF-G

Maddox, John D. ~ 19INF-G

Maddox, Madison ~ 19INF-G

Mann, William G. ~ 44INF-I

Martin, J. H. ~ 44INF-I

Massey, Thomas ~ 19INF-G

Masters, Griffin S. ~ 22INF-K

Masters, William J. ~ 44INF-I

Mathews, R. B. (or Osborn S.) ~ 44INF-I

Mathews, William O. ~ 44INF-I

McCarthy, James ~ 44INF-I

McClelland, James M. ~ 44INF-I

McClelland, John F. ~ 44INF-I

McClelland, William R. ~ 44INF-I

McCord, William H. H. ~ 19INF-G

McCoy, William T. ~ 44INF-I

McCulley, James C. ~ 22INF-K

McDaniel Simeon C. ~ 19INF-G

McElroy, Jesse ~ 44INF-I

McGarity, Jeremiah A. ~ 22INF-K

McGarity, John M. ~ 22INF-K

McGarity, Thomas F. ~ 22INF-K

McKee, Madison Church ~ 22INF-K

McKee, Samuel Payne ~ 22INF-K

McKenzie, Augustus D. ~ 44INF-A

McMullen, Jeremiah A. ~ 44INF-I

McMullen, Sanford W. ~ 44INF-I

Merritt, William Parks ~ 19INF-G

Mills, R. L. ~ 44INF-A

Minter, Richard H. ~ 44INF-A

Mobley, William F. ~ 19INF-G

Moore, Charles W. ~ 44INF-A

Moore, Henry M. ~ 44INF-A

Moore, James ~ 44INF-A

Moore, Jesse G. ~ 44INF-A

Moore, Robert ~ 44INF-A

Moore, Robert A. ~ 44INF-A

Moore, Sanford R. ~ 44INF-A

Moore, Thomas S. (or Thomas L.) ~ 44INF-A

Morgan, Jesse M. ~ 44INF-I

Morris, Darling D. ~ 19INF-G

Morris, Joseph T. ~ 44INF-I

Morris, Robert Newton ~ 44INF-I

Morris, William Jasper ~ 44INF-A

Morton, William J. ~ 44INF-I

Moseley, John W. ~ 19INF-G

Moseley, Josephus ~ 19INF-G

Moseley, Peter G. ~ 19INF-G

Moseley, William T. ~ 19INF-G
Mosley, Henry S. ~ 22INF-K
Moss, William J. ~ 44INF-I
Murray, George T. ~ 44INF-I
Murray, James M. ~ 44INF-I
Nix, J. Allman ~ 22INF-K
Nix, John J. ~ 22INF-K
Nixon, William J. ~ 44INF-A
Nolley, Timen M. ~ 22INF-K
Norris, John E. ~ 22INF-K
Oglesby, George H.(Tobe) ~ 19INF-G
Oglesby, Gus ~ 19INF-G
Oglesby, Robert L ~ 19INF-G
Oglesby, Silas Moseley. ~ 19INF-G
Orr, John S. ~ 44INF-A
Orr, Noah ~ 44INF-I
Owen, Emory M. (or Owens) ~ 22INF-K
Owen, J. S. (or Owens) ~ 22INF-K
Owen, Newsom T. (or Owens) ~ 22INF-K
Owen, Westley C. (or Owens) ~ 22INF-K
Owen, William H. ~ 19INF-G
Owens, Augustus ~ 19INF-G
Paschal, Richard H. C. ~ 44INF-I
Pattillo, Benjamin H. ~ 22INF-K
Pattillo, George M. T. ~ 22INF-K
Pattillo, James M. ~ 22INF-K
Pattillo, John R. J. ~ 22INF-K
Pattillo, Silas L. ~ 44INF-I

Peebles, Henry H. ~ 44INF-A
Peebles, John T. ~ 44INF-A
Peebles, William H. ~ 44INF-A
Pendley, John M. ~ 44INF-A
Pendley, William Jasper ~ 44INF-A
Perryman, Freeman W. ~ 44INF-I
Phillips, Arrington ~ 19INF-G
Phillips, Crawford ~ 44INF-A
Phillips, David ~ 44INF-A
Phillips, Hardy ~ 19INF-G
Phillips, Harris Jesse ~ 22INF-K
Phillips, James R. ~ 19INF-G
Phillips, James W. ~ 44INF-A
Phillips, John A. ~ 19INF-G
Phillips, John G. ~ 19INF-G
Phillips, Robert B. ~ 19INF-G
Phillips, W. C. ~ 19INF-G
Phillips, William A. ~ 22INF-K
Pierce, William B. ~ 44INF-A
Ponder, George M. ~ 44INF-A
Pope, Joel Crawford ~ 22INF-K
Pope, W. F. ~ 22INF-K
Powell, James T. ~ 44INF-I
Price, W. T. ~ 44INF-A
Price, William C. ~ 44INF-A
Pritchett, John W. ~ 22INF-K
Privates: ~ 19INF-G
Puckett, John A. ~ 19INF-G
Pullin, Jeptha Polk ~ 44INF-A
Ragan, James H. ~ 22INF-K
Rape, Milton A. ~ 19INF-G
Rape, Peter ~ 19INF-G
Rawls, John ~ 44INF-A
Rawls, William ~ 44INF-A

Ray, Thomas N. ~ 22INF-K
Ray, W. W. ~ 22INF-K
Reeves, Abner ~ 44INF-I
Richards, John R. (or John A.)
~ 19INF-G
Richards, John R. (or John A.)
~ 22INF-K
Richardson, Robert B. ~
44INF-A
Richardson, William M. ~
44INF-A
Riley, James M. ~ 44INF-I
Riley, William M. ~ 22INF-K
Roberts, David O. ~ 44INF-I
Roberts, William H. ~ 44INF-I
Robertson, Alonzo G. ~
44INF-I
Robertson, Bennett B. ~
22INF-K
Robertson, Noel R. (or Novell
R.) ~ 22INF-K
Robertson, Wilson L. ~ 44INF-
I
Rosser, John A. ~ 44INF-A
Rowan, Abraham Alex ~
19INF-G
Rowden, Elijah A. ~ 19INF-G
Rowland, Berry (or Roland) ~
44INF-I
Russell, John ~ 44INF-A
Salter, William ~ 44INF-A
Sappington, David M. ~
22INF-K
Sappington, James H. ~
44INF-I
Sappington, John T. ~ 44INF-I
Selfridge, John R. ~ 19INF-G
Setzer, John ~ 19INF-G

Shaw, Eugenius N. ~ 44INF-I
Shaw, J. M. ~ 44INF-A
Shaw, James W. ~ 44INF-A
Sherrer, James T. ~ 19INF-G
Simpkins, James H. ~ 22INF-K
Simpkins, Robert B. ~ 22INF-K
Simpson, James A. ~ 22INF-K
Sims, Cicero H. ~ 19INF-G
Sims, James N. ~ 22INF-K
Skelton, Charles S. ~ 22INF-K
Skinner, H. J. ~ 22INF-K
Smith, Ferdinand R. (or
Fernanders R.) ~ 44INF-I
Smith, James M. ~ 44INF-I
Smith, John C. ~ 22INF-K
Smith, Joseph J. ~ 44INF-A
Smith, Levi J. ~ 44INF-I
Smith, Sidney H. ~ 19INF-G
Smith, William Jasper ~
44INF-A
Smith, William Jasper ~
44INF-I
Snidler, Thompson D. T. ~
44INF-A
Snow, James Marion ~
44INF-A
Sorrow, F. L. ~ 22INF-K
South, Francis C. ~ 44INF-I
South, Newton M. ~ 44INF-I
Sowell, John Perry ~ 44INF-A
Sowell, Martin Van Buren ~
44INF-A
Speer, James H. ~ 19INF-G
Speer, Joseph H. C. (Sug) ~
19INF-G

Sprayberry, Ferdinand G. ~ 22INF-K

Sprayberry, Robert E. ~ 22INF-K

Sprayberry, Uphrates A. V. ~ 22INF-K

Stancell, John N. (or Stansell) ~ 44INF-A

Stanfield, Abner L. ~ 44INF-A

Stanfield, John H. ~ 44INF-A

Stanfield, William M. ~ 44INF-A

Stanley, A. J. ~ 22INF-K

Stanley, Bithum L ~ 22INF-K

Stanley, Eli ~ 22INF-K

Stanley, J. B. ~ 22INF-K

Stanley, J. G. ~ 22INF-K

Stanley, Jesse ~ 22INF-K

Stanley, John J. ~ 22INF-K

Stanley, John M. ~ 22INF-K

Stanley, Laudrick (or Loderick) ~ 22INF-K

Stanley, Levi ~ 22INF-K

Stanley, William B. ~ 22INF-K

Stanton, John H. ~ 44INF-I

Stapp, Henry J. ~ 44INF-I

Stapp, Solomon J. ~ 44INF-I

Stapp, Thomas W. J. ~ 44INF-I

Stark, Thomas P. J. ~ 44INF-I

Steighan, Frederick ~ 19INF-G

Stephens, William Rufus ~ 22INF-K

Stephenson, William M. ~ 22INF-K

Stewart, J. M. ~ 22INF-K

Stewart, John M ~ 19INF-G

Stokes, Henry ~ 19INF-G

Street, Francis M. ~ 44INF-A

Streeter, Joseph ~ 44INF-I

Strickland, Leroy ~ 44INF-A

Sykes, Jacob ~ 19INF-G

Sykes, Thomas M. Y. ~ 19INF-G

Sykes, W. L. ~ 22INF-K

Tanner, Josiah G. ~ 22INF-K

Tarpley, Henry C. ~ 44INF-A

Tarpley, Lucius M. ~ 44INF-A

Tarpley, William Hamp ~ 44INF-A

Taylor, John R. ~ 19INF-G

Teel, Alvin ~ 19INF-G

Thompson, Alfred ~ 44INF-A

Thompson, James E. ~ 19INF-G

Thompson, Joseph ~ 19INF-G

Thompson, Lemuel Harris ~ 22INF-K

Thompson, Samuel M. ~ 22INF-K

Thompson, Wiley ~ 44INF-A

Thurman, John Michael ~ 19INF-G

Tidwell, M. M. ~ 19INF-G

Tidwell, Mathew M. ~ 22INF-K

Tomlin, A. J. ~ 44INF-I

Tomlin, Milton L. ~ 44INF-I

Tomlin, Newton J. ~ 44INF-I

Tomlinson, John I. (or John J. ~ 19INF-G

Tomlinson, Joseph P ~ 19INF-G

Tomlinson, William ~ 19INF-G

Townsend, John L ~ 19INF-G
Townsend, John L. ~ 22INF-K
Townsend, Littleton Dennis ~ 22INF-K
Townsend, Odum L ~ 22INF-K
Turner, Charles ~ 44INF-A
Turner, David T. ~ 44INF-A
Turner, Hilliard A. ~ 44INF-A
Turner, John J. ~ 44INF-A
Turner, Joseph S. ~ 44INF-A
Turner, M. T. ~ 44INF-A
Turner, Peyton S. ~ 44INF-A
Turnipseed, Jesse C. ~ 44INF-A
Turnipseed, John W. ~ 44INF-A
Turnipseed, Nathaniel C. ~ 44INF-A
Underwood, Melbourn B. ~ 19INF-G
Underwood, William M. ~ 19INF-G
Upchurch, Alfred V. ~ 19INF-G
Upchurch, James M. ~ 44INF-A
Upchurch, Jasper ~ 44INF-A
Upchurch, Lloyd A. ~ 44INF-A
Varner, William D. ~ 19INF-G
Walden, Robert, Jr. (or Waldin) ~ 22INF-K
Waldrup, J. C. ~ 22INF-K
Walker, Americus V. (or Americus E.) ~ 19INF-G
Walker, Andrew W. ~ 19INF-G
Walker, George Washington ~ 19INF-G
Walker, Rufus John ~ 44INF-I
Walker, Silas L ~ 19INF-G
Wallace, Simeon S. ~ 22INF-K
Ward, Edward M. T. ~ 19INF-G
Weems, Gilbert G. ~ 44INF-A
Weems, James R. ~ 44INF-A
Weems, John R. ~ 44INF-A
Weems, John Walker ~ 44INF-A
Weems, John Wesley ~ 44INF-A
Whitaker, William H. ~ 19INF-G
White, David T. ~ 44INF-I
White, John W. ~ 22INF-K
White, Thomas A. ~ 22INF-K
Whitley, Francis N. ~ 22INF-K
Whitley, Marion W. ~ 22INF-K
Whooten, William A. ~ 44INF-I
Wilder, Larkin ~ 19INF-G
Wilkins, Samuel J. ~ 44INF-A
Wilkins, William J. ~ 44INF-A
Wilkinson, ~ 19INF-G
Wilkinson, Joseph N. ~ 22INF-K
Wilkinson, Robert M. ~ 22INF-K
Williams, James M. ~ 44INF-A
Williams, John R. ~ 19INF-G
Wilson, Augustus J. ~ 22INF-K
Wilson, David ~ 22INF-K
Wilson, William S. (or William L.) ~ 44INF-A

Winfrey, Thomas E. ~ 44INF-I

Wise, George E. ~ 19INF-G

Wise, J. D. R. ~ 19INF-G

Wood, John W. ~ 44INF-I

Woods, Winchester ~ 44INF-I

Wright, William J. ~ 44INF-A

Wyatt, Frank ~ 44INF-A

Wyatt, George W. ~ 44INF-A

Wyatt, S. J. ~ 19INF-G

Youngblood, Cincinnatus ~ 44INF-I

Zachry, Clementius R. ~ 44INF-I

Made in the USA
San Bernardino, CA
14 March 2017